ACPL ITEM
DISCARDED
SO-AUF-871

796.52
Gabbard, Andrea
Mountaineering

A Ragged Mountain Press
WOMAN'S GUIDE

MOUNTAINEERING

ANDREA GABBARD

Series Editor, Molly Mulhern Gross

RAGGED MOUNTAIN PRESS/ McGRAW HILL

Camden, Maine • New York • San Francisco • Washington, D.C. • Auckland
Bogotá • Caracas • Lisbon • London • Madrid • Mexico City • Milan
Montreal • New Delhi • San Juan • Singapore • Sydney • Tokyo • Toronto

Look for these other Ragged Mountain Press Woman's Guides

Sea Kayaking, Shelley Johnson
Backpacking, Adrienne Hall
Snowboarding, Julia Carlson
Fly Fishing, Dana Rikimaru

Sailing, Doris Colgate
Canoeing, Laurie Gullion
Skiing, Maggie Loring
Winter Sports, Iseult Devlin

● ●

Allen County Public Library
900 Webster Street
PO Box 2270
Fort Wayne, IN 46801-2270

Ragged Mountain Press

A Division of The McGraw·Hill Companies

10 9 8 7 6 5 4 3 2 1
Copyright © 1999 by Andrea Gabbard
All rights reserved. The publisher takes no responsibility for the use of any of the materials or
methods described in this book, nor for the products thereof. The name "Ragged Mountain Press"
and the Ragged Mountain Press logo are trademarks of The McGraw-Hill Companies.
Printed in the United States of America.

Library of Congress Cataloging-in-Publication Data
Gabbard, Andrea,
    Mountaineering/Andrea Gabbard.
       p. cm.—(A Ragged Mountain Press woman's guide)
    Includes bibliographical references (p. 115) and index.
    ISBN 0-07-103402-1 (alk. paper)
    1. Mountaineering—Washington (State)—Rainier, Mount.
      2. Rainer, Mount (Wash.) 3. Mountaineers—United States—Biography.
      4. Women mountaineers—United States—Biography. I. Title. II. Series
GV199.42.w22r343 1999
796.52'2'09797782—dc21
                                     98-41573
                                      CIP

Questions regarding the content of this book
should be addressed to:
  Ragged Mountain Press
  P.O. Box 220, Camden, ME 04843
  www.raggedmountainpress.com

Questions regarding the ordering of this book
should be addressed to:
  The McGraw-Hill Companies
  Customer Service Department
  P.O. Box 547, Blacklick, OH 43004
  Retail customers: 1-800-262-4729
  Bookstores: 1-800-722-4726

Printed by Quebecor Printing Co., Fairfield, PA
Edited by Connie Burt
Design by Carol Inouye, Inkstone Communications Design
Project management by Janet Robbins
Page layout by Shannon Thomas
Credits and permission to use quoted material may be found on
page 127.

Warning: This is an instructional book for potentially dangerous activities. Mountaineering and ice climbing may subject you to climbing falls; rock and ice falls; avalanches; injuries from exposure, such as frostbite and hypothermia; and many other hazards that can lead to serious injury and death. This book is not intended to replace instruction by a qualified instructor nor to substitute for your personal judgment. In using this book, the reader releases the author, publisher, and distributor from liability for any injury, including death, that might result.

•••••••••••••••••••••••••••••••

"The journey is what matters.
The summit is an arbitrary
place to turn around."

—Heather MacDonald

•••••••••••••••••••••••••••••••

Why do they climb?"
The question came up in my reading group's discussion of the mountaineers portrayed in a new but already popular climbing narrative.

"Why not?" I returned, obviously the only woman in the room dreaming of snow-covered summits and predawn calls to don headlamps and crampons and head for the peak.

But indeed, why would I think of climbing Mount Rainier? What is so compelling about such a quest—one that requires months of physical and mental preparation—and one in which the outcome is so utterly outside my ability to control? (When was the last time you had a good guarantee from the weather?) Well, maybe it is just that mixture of physical challenge, personal focus, teamwork, and faithfulness—in the mountain, the rope team, and my own self—that entices me.

I've backpacked over many mountains, but except for hiking across glaciers in Glacier National Park as a five-year-old, I've never done any mountaineering—and I wouldn't have given it a second thought until my sister climbed Mount Rainier a few years ago. I still remember her call after their aborted summit attempt: "We had to turn around: one team member was pretty weak and the weather was moving in," she explained. For the first time I realized that my sister had been involved in serious adventure, a test of will and stamina unlike anything I had ever imagined. My curiosity was piqued. I hadn't known that Rainier was that kind of a mountain, full of crevasses, glaciers, and the perils of the Himalayan peaks I'd been fascinated with since childhood.

Once while standing at Paradise—the settlement at 5,400 feet that is the most popular starting point for climbing Rainier—I watched longingly as otherworldly-seeming athletes hoisted packs and headed up the well-worn trail toward Camp Muir, a base camp that appears as a mere speck from the visitors' center. I wanted to know what they were headed for and just what it took for them to climb that far-off peak. My sister's call rekindled that fascination.

And you know what? That journey to Camp Muir and that mountain peak don't seem as daunting anymore. It's not because suddenly I'm an alpinist, but because of the book you're holding. You see, *Mountaineering: A Woman's Guide* answers some of the questions I had about what those climbers were doing and about what it takes to climb that mountain. Andrea Gabbard has climbed Rainier several times, and in this book she's collected lots of inspiration and advice to help you get out and summit your own peaks. Here you'll hear Andrea's and other women's mountaineering experiences—and they range far beyond Mount Rainier—told in a manner that respects how women learn and grow.

What's so different about the way women learn? If you're like me, you like to hear a description or an overview of a move or tactic before launching into it. I guess you could say I'm a fan of the "talk-it-over-and-think-it-through-first" school of outdoor learning. I want to ask questions about the self-arrest technique before I'm asked to rope into a harness, connect to a team of other climbers, and pitch myself down a snow-covered slope (see page 75 for Andrea's advice). I want to hear advice from someone who is like me, someone I know and trust. And I benefit from learning in a group, because I hear other folks' questions—and discover I'm not the only one wondering how to strap on those crampons (see page 71)! We've done our best to mimic these learning conditions in The Ragged Mountain Press Woman's Guides. *Mountaineering: A Woman's Guide* provides solutions, advice, and stories from women who have summitted peaks near and far. I hope Andrea's words and approach help get you out to explore and enjoy, with a guide or with experienced friends. I'll look for you out there.

When you get a break from your mountain journeys, drop us a note to tell us how we're doing and how we can improve these guides to best suit you and your learning style.

MOLLY MULHERN GROSS
Series Editor, The Ragged Mountain Press Woman's Guides
Camden, Maine
December 1998

An avid outdoorswoman, Molly Mulhern Gross enjoys running, hiking, camping, sea kayaking, telemark skiing, in-line skating, and biking and has just started snowboarding. She is Director of Editing, Design, and Production at Ragged Mountain Press and International Marine.

CONTENTS

CONTENTS

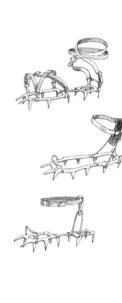

Acknowledgments

This book would not have been possible without the dedication and cooperation of Francey Blaugrund and Terry Austin; the assistance of Lou and Peter Whittaker of Rainier Mountaineering, Inc.; and the expertise of RMI senior guide Heather MacDonald and the other RMI guides who assisted her during the seminar: Chris Booher, Matt Hartman, Paul Maier, and Tap Richards.

Appreciation is also extended to seminar climbers Bonnie Pene, Kevin Braun, Dan Courtney, Ted Curcio, Carlos Feldman, Scott McDonald, Joseph Murphy, Ron Rehfuss, Michael Schultz, Brian Slyman, and Michael Walenta. May all your future journeys be safe and successful!

For her encouragement, patience, flexibility, and vision, I thank my editor at Ragged Mountain Press, Molly Mulhern Gross; for lending their excellent copyediting skills, Dorcas S. Miller and Constance G. Burt; and thanks also to Keith Gunnar for photography and Kurt Wedberg for "Great Mountains" recommendations.

We also extend our appreciation to the companies that outfitted Francey and Terry from head to toe, including Backpacker's Pantry, Cascade Designs, Climb High/Julbo, JanSport, Leki, Lowa, Lowe Alpine Systems, Marmot Mountain Ltd., Moving Comfort, Mountainsmith, Outdoor Research, Patagonia, PMI/Petzl, Sierra Designs, Smart Wool, Seattle Manufacturing Company, and The North Face.

And to the many women whose experiences are captured in words and spirit in these pages—including Heather MacDonald, Arlene Blum, Stacy Allison, Heidi Howkins, Jennifer Herzig, Leah Hall, Helen Thayer, Amber M. Brookman, Barbara Harris, Christine Janin, Ruth Anne Kocour, Maureen O'Neill, Margo Chisholm, and Fay Fuller—thank you for helping pave the way for other women.

ANDREA GABBARD
Oakhurst, California
December 1998

On August 9, 1890, Fay Fuller prepared to hike up a mountain she had longed to climb—Mount Tahoma, now called Rainier. She drove brads into the soles of her boots so they would hold in ice and snow and rubbed her face with charcoal to blunt the sun's rays. She wore a long woolen dress and woolen hose, and slung over her shoulder a bedroll of two blankets, food for three days, and a canteen. She seized her alpenstock and "resolved to climb until exhausted."

Fay Fuller braved the cold, the wind, and the dangers of the glaciers. On August 10, she and her four male companions climbed up to the rim of the crater and then went on to the top of the mountain. She was the first woman to climb Mount Rainier. Her effort is all the more astounding in light of the fact that modern mountaineers consider the 14,411-foot mountain in Washington State the longest endurance climb in the Continental United States. They come from all over the world to train for major expeditions on Rainier, for it offers conditions similar to those found on the world's highest peaks.

Situated in the direct path of moist maritime air from the Pacific Ocean, Rainier is famous for its fickle weather, summer or winter. Storms can blow in within minutes and clear just as rapidly, or lay siege to the mountain for days. The mountain's glaciated flanks (Rainier is host to 27 glaciers) provide all the challenges of mixed terrain that mountaineers crave: rock, ice, and snow. Yawning crevasses scar the upper reaches. As the glaciers expand and contract, great chunks of ice break free and tumble onto the snowfields below or form towering, pointed masses of ice called seracs—enticing routes for technical ice climbers.

A hundred years after Fay Fuller realized her goal, I, too, set out to climb Mount Rainier. On my first two attempts, my physical strength peaked out far below the summit. On the next two forays, the weather thwarted my aspirations. The fifth time, my climbing party was blessed with an unprecedented five days of clear and sunny weather, and I stood on the highest point of the summit crater enjoying a 360-degree view of the surrounding mountains and Puget Sound in the distance. I didn't want to come down! The sixth time, in June 1996, my party was forced to turn back 800 feet below the summit in a whiteout blizzard. In the process of flinging myself against Mount Rainier's flanks (and on subsequent climbs of mountains in South America and Africa), I have learned many lessons—about mountains, life, and myself. That's why I keep going back.

For me, mountain climbing is a metaphor for life experience. You set a goal—in this instance, the summit—and then ascend, one step at a time, toward that goal without guarantee of success. During the journey, you learn and perfect skills, experience challenges, and encounter obstacles. Along the way, your perspective may change with each new vantage point. Mental and physical powers are put to the test. Survival often hinges on a serendipitous change in attitude—

yours or the mountain's. Mountaineers are fond of this oft-quoted, non-attributed observation: "Life does not happen on the summit. Life is what happens on the sides of the mountain." Mountain climbing offers an important lesson: It's the journey that matters.

My first mountaineering experience was recent enough that I remember what it's like to be a beginner. I recall the first time I strapped on my crampons (a frame of metal spikes attached to mountaineering boots to provide more traction on snow and ice), the first time I looked into the abyss of a crevasse (or hole) in a glacier, the first time fear gnawed at the pit of my stomach. I like to think that I'm qualified to introduce you to the world of mountaineering because I do remember. I won't gloss over the difficulties or portray the trip as a macho challenge. You'll hear my voice and also the voices of lots of other women who have taken up this sport. I hope that these women will inform you, encourage you, and give you the energy to fulfill your own dream.

I advise anyone without mountaineering experience to seek expert instruction before venturing onto higher ground. You may be fortunate enough to have a skilled and experienced friend who can be your personal guide. Or you may choose to learn to climb with a professional guide or at a climbing school.

In this book, I take you on a guided trip featuring two women—43-year-old Francey Blaugrund and 32-year-old Terry Austin—neither of whom had any previous mountaineering experience. Heather MacDonald, senior guide at Rainier Mountaineering, Inc. (RMI), leads Francey and Terry (and the rest of us) on an expedition up Rainier. We go step by step, covering training, clothing, equipment, techniques—and all the joys and apprehensions, the exhilaration and exhaustion that accompany any climb.

Chapter 1

THE FEMALE MOUNTAINEER

What is the difference between hiking or backpacking in the mountains and mountaineering? Both involve potentially dangerous weather, rough terrain, and health emergencies. In general, backpacking is done on non-technical terrain with a minimum of technical skills required. Mountaineering calls for a wider repertoire of skills—including specific breathing and walking methods—to move up or across steep expanses of snow, ice, or rock. Such mountaineering skills usually call for the use of ropes, crampons, ice axes, and other specialty tools and implements. At altitudes over 24,000 feet, supplemental oxygen is commonly used by mountaineers to facilitate breathing and to help prevent frostbite, hypothermia, and altitude sickness.

In both backpacking and mountaineering, good judgment is essential. The safety of the group is as important as the safety of each individual. Whereas backpackers sometimes hike above tree level, mountaineers regularly venture into high, desolate environments where the effects of extreme cold, vicious snowstorms, and lack of atmospheric pressure increase the risk of contracting life-threatening ailments such as pulmonary edema, cerebral edema, and hypothermia. In mountaineering, the margin for error can be small indeed.

This book is intended to give you an idea of what mountaineering is all about and what will be required of you to participate. It does not describe every situation you might encounter in the mountains, nor does it pretend to give you all you need to know to become a proficient moun-

• •

"In our quest for physical comfort, we often neglect our spiritual need to honestly and openly confront both our own mortality and the fragility of our world. We pad all of the sharp edges in our lives with bleached cotton or high-tech foam, and then wonder why the notion of a wild wind whipping across an exposed ridge both terrifies and fascinates us. We deny our kids real challenges, guarantee that they'll move from grade to grade, and then wonder why they respond with apathy and indifference. We travel to work in climate-controlled vehicles and spend the day in a gray cubicle, and then wonder why we crave caffeine and other artificial stimulants."

—Professional climber Heidi Howkins, age 30;
excerpt from her essay,
"Kangchenjunga: Passages in Ice"

• •

taineer on your own. Such proficiency takes time, many climbs, many mountains—and that's the fun part! Each climb is unique; each climb offers a new experience.

WHY TAKE UP MOUNTAINEERING?

Every woman has her own reason. Some seek out the physical challenge, some want the mental challenge, some look for the aesthetic rewards that come from ascending the peaks. Stacy Allison was the first American woman to stand on the summit of Mount Everest. In her book, *Beyond the Limits*, she explains why she climbs mountains: "I climb because *I'm* here. I don't battle the mountains. I don't conquer anything, even when I do pull myself onto a summit. For me the triumph comes in every step, in every breath and heartbeat. It's the sheer pleasure of being on the planet, of seeing the mountains around me and, for a brief moment, being a part of them. My spirit leaps, my voice joins the heavenly chorus of the living. I climb for a simple reason: because I'm alive."

French climber Christine Janin, the first woman to ascend the highest peak on each of the seven continents, identifies a different feeling: freedom. After climbing in Antarctica, Janin recounted, "It was always windy, a white void. At night, I could see the polar lights. They instilled in me a great sensation of liberty. When my team and I reached the top of an unclimbed peak, I experienced a phenomenal sense of freedom. It was a gift."

Artist and recreational climber Ruth Anne Kocour was on a guided climb of Alaska's 20,320-foot Mount McKinley in 1992 when her climbing party became trapped at 14,000 feet by a massive storm. The party was tentbound for nearly two weeks while the storm blanketed the mountain in raging winds, unrelenting blizzards, and extreme sub-zero temperatures. When the storm lifted, the group decided to risk a summit attempt—and made it. In her book about the experience, *Facing the Extreme*, Kocour recalls her moment of triumph: "I was calm, peaceful, acutely aware of everything past and present and the interconnection of things—that nature is not something outside ourselves, but who we are. I marveled at what once seemed important, such as possessions, plans. . . . Here, high above the mayhem of the world, I found myself reminded that it's not how much we have, but how little we need, that counts."

In *Annapurna, A Woman's Place*, Arlene Blum writes that getting to the top of Annapurna brought rewards far beyond knowing that they had been the first Americans and the first all-women team to climb the mountain. "Looking up at the remote summit, it was hard to believe that any of us had ever stood there, even harder to comprehend the great loss that accompanied our achievement. But we had gained something more than the summit. The years of planning and the months of climbing together had changed and strengthened us. We had survived the hardest physical and psychological stresses, and found that as a team we could do great things. . . . In addition, we had gained the friendship and warmth that now united us. . . . For me, this was as important as having reached the summit."

"What I love about mountaineering is that it causes you to think positively. The incredible danger of what you're doing flashes through your mind, but you can't afford to think about it. This is such a powerful learning experience that translates directly to everyday life. In dealing with adversity, you have to focus all your energies on the positive."

—Barbara Harris, Editor-in-Chief, *Shape* magazine

In 1994, I journeyed to Bolivia to climb 19,870-foot Huayna Potosi, a classic pyramid-shaped peak with a 500-foot, 50-degree headwall leading to the summit. It was my first adventure over 14,000 feet. I had acclimatized well until we reached our high camp at 18,000 feet. There, I found it hard to breathe and impossible to sleep. The night before our summit attempt was an epic of fear. I felt suffocated by the lack of oxygen. I'd repeatedly doze off, then jerk awake, gasping and gulping for air. I couldn't get warm, I couldn't sleep, all I could think was, "How am I ever going to climb to the summit?"

Early the next morning, the guide came by to make sure that my tentmate and I were awake and ready to go. I said, "Pete, I don't think I can do this. I didn't get any sleep last night. I feel pretty yucky." He glanced at me and said, "Whatever you decide, Andrea. Depends on how badly you want it," and walked away. My friend, Pete, left me alone to battle my own fears and self-pity.

Actually, his response pissed me off, which is exactly what he intended. I got dressed, drank a quart of water, ate a granola bar, and instantly felt better. I stuffed gear into my pack, grabbed my ice axe, and started moving around, getting my blood moving, and felt even

Andrea Gabbard in Bolivia, with 19,870-foot Huayna Potosi in background.

better. By the time we had hiked about a half-hour up the glacier, I felt strong and very motivated. When I reached the summit, I gave Pete a big thank-you hug . . . and myself a few pats on the back for summoning the courage to move into the unknown. The endless view of the surrounding snow-capped Andes and the precipitous perch of the knife-edge summit were breathtakingly memorable. If I had stayed behind in my tent, I would have missed another indelible gift from the mountain.

HOW AND WHY THEY GOT STARTED

Heather MacDonald, who guides us up Mount Rainier in this book, started climbing at age 15 when she was in Europe on a student-exchange program. "I went to Mont Blanc," she recalls. "It was the first time I had ever held an ice axe or worn crampons. It felt huge to me. I knew immediately that I would be doing this."

She selected a college in Portland, Oregon, where she would be near the great mountains of the Pacific Northwest. "I climbed Mount Rainier for the first time when I was 17. I summited and then later that year took a winter seminar. By the time I was 20, I was working as a guide."

Jennifer Herzig, a mountaineer and high-school teacher, relates that her mother helped her realize her dream. "For high-school graduation, my mother gave me a climb of Mount Rainier, a mountain that I had wanted to climb since I was seven years old. Out of seven clients, I was the only woman. I had been very athletic in high school, but this climb was the hardest thing I had ever done. On summit day, I felt so terrible I couldn't eat or drink. I made it to the top, but I was crying, I felt so awful. One of the guides made me eat a few cookies. He said, 'You'll feel 100 percent better in an hour.' He was absolutely right. When I came off the mountain, I was sore, but I had forgotten how miserable I had been. That was it. I was hooked."

There are also women who started mountaineering much later in their lives. I was 40 when I first ventured onto Mount Rainier, and one notable woman from the past, Annie Peck, did her first climb when she was almost that age. Annie Peck went on to make her mark in the mountains. In 1895, she became the third woman to climb the Matterhorn in Europe (shocking the public because she wore knickerbockers instead of a dress), and in 1908—at the age of 58—she made the first ascent of the North Peak of Mount Huascaran, a 21,812-foot peak in Peru.

DIFFERENCES BETWEEN WOMEN AND MEN

Heather MacDonald has guided both women and men and believes that women experience climbing in a different way than men do. "Men see climbing as a battle or a war. They're out to conquer the mountain, which is so ridiculous and ego-driven. If you let go of your ego, you can go so much farther. Your ego takes you in the wrong direction and closes your heart. Women's hearts are so much more expanded and open. Women 'get it' a lot sooner: We're here on a mountain, we're working with it, relating to it."

Heidi Howkins, a 30-year-old professional climber, says it this way: "You can see the difference in how men and women approach mountain climbing during a trek to base camp.

Women want to interact with the culture, talk to the people, hold the babies. Men check their altimeters, go over the route maps, check gear."

While it is dangerous to rely too heavily on generalizations—not all men are out to conquer the mountain, and all mountaineers should go over maps and check gear at some point—it is important to remember that you need not measure yourself against some prototype image of the perfect (manly) mountaineer.

A recent finding about physiology may be of interest to women mountaineers. Two types of muscle come into play when engaging in adventure sports: Fast-twitch muscle provides power, while slow-twitch muscle provides endurance. Research has shown that, on average, women tend to have a higher percentage of slow-twitch "endurance" muscle than men. This long-term capacity can pay dividends because mountaineering is more of an endurance than a power sport.

"I'm an experienced rock climber. What frightens me about mountaineering is that I become a novice again. In situations of nearly vertical and high exposure I really experience fear. There aren't that many situations in my life where I experience that type of fear. I love that challenge because of what it requires me to do. I feel all the fears of a novice and have to deal with this awkwardness and lack of knowledge. I have to exercise patience to acquire skills and to acquire the confidence that I can persist and learn."

— Barbara Harris

THE FEAR FACTOR

Have you ever been in a situation where you or someone in your group has become hysterical or paralyzed by fear? Most often, this occurs from fear of the unknown. The more you learn about proper mountaineering technique and mountain safety, the less likely you will become "too afraid." And, the more experienced you become in the mountains, the more likely you will be able to extract yourself or a climbing partner from a dangerous situation. Your fears may always stay with you, but they will begin to work in your favor.

"Risk and real danger are an important part of the high-altitude climbing game," says Heidi Howkins. "There is something essential about the possibility of real loss, even death, in the game, and without the presence of danger many climbers would quit. Honing your ice-climbing skills on a two-story ice cube simply isn't the same as climbing, creeping, up a delicate, unstable icefall, where many two-story ice cubes can topple on you at any time. The first of these two activities leaves you with the pride of self-discipline and the warm glow of accomplishment. The second leaves you with that hair-raising, skin-crawling sense of how evanescent achievement is, how puny your own little dance is when compared with the sheer mass of motion in the cosmos."

• •

"**M**ountaineering has taught me to live simply, to stay focused and have patience. When I returned from Everest, using flush toilets and drinking from a glass seemed like luxuries. Going without a shower for two months—it's hard to explain to friends what an experience that is."

—Jennifer Herzig

• •

Maureen O'Neill, a climber and author of "Queen of All She Surveys" in the book *Leading Out*, explains fear this way: "To the climber, fear serves several purposes. It can make you attentive to possible danger, can warn you, infuse you with energy, serve as a gauge of your mental condition, and prevent you from taking risks beyond your ability. . . . The natural flow of fear must be channeled or paralysis can result, and paralysis is serious. For me, fear manifests through resistance and hesitation, both of which cause unnecessary energy loss."

Fear is a natural and very real emotion. In December 1992, Christine Janin, the French climber who ascended the highest peak on each of the seven continents, admitted in an interview that she was sometimes "very afraid" when climbing, but added, "If you're too afraid, you might make a fatal mistake. I've never been so afraid that I've cried." She had surmounted many of her fears through her experience in the mountains.

Heather MacDonald has some insights of her own. "A lot of people climb to confront their fears. And even though it manifests itself in mountain terms—exposure, a crevasse, weather—I think climbers, in confronting their fears this way, work out a lot of other things they're fearful of in their everyday lives. Fear comes in different forms, but 99 percent of the time, the root of fear is self-doubt."

Like other mountaineers, she has had to deal with fear. "In 1994, the first time I was on Mount Everest, it wasn't so much fear for my life, but fear of failure. To me, that's fear in the first degree. I was 24 and one of the guides on a commercial climb. There were two climbers on the upper mountain. One of them had just descended from the summit. One was in trouble. We had sent a guide up to help him. I was at Camp V (about 24,500 feet) with two other clients and another guide, Bob. He went up to assist the other client while I helped the two clients at camp prepare to descend. The expedition leader called me on the radio and told me to send my radio down with the clients, and then go up and help Bob with the other climber.

"I'd never been that high before. I'd made the mistake of not studying the route, but the leader said that I shouldn't have a problem finding it because there would be a lot of fixed rope on that particular route. I was determined to give it my best shot. I loaded up my backpack and climbed up to the top of the snowfield at 26,000 feet. There was fresh snow and I couldn't see any fixed rope. Here I am without a radio because I had sent it down with the two clients.

"I'm looking at three or four gullies, and I can't remember which one it is. I thought I knew which was the right one—later, I learned my hunch was right—and I started going up, then came down, thinking, 'What if I get lost?' I had no way of letting anyone know where I was. I felt very uncomfortable. So I started back down to camp.

"Then I thought, 'No, I can't fail those guys, they need me,' and headed back up. This went on for an hour, starting up, going back down. Finally, I sat down on my pack and said, 'Heather, what have you always done when you're not sure? You've listened to the mountain.' So I turned around and faced the summit. At that elevation, it seems like it's *right there*. And real clearly, the mountain said, 'Go away, little girl. You're strong and you think you're ready to be at 29,000 feet, but you're not.'

> "**I** wonder if the real definition of courage is the ability to deal successfully with one's fears. At the end of this expedition, I hope to be not only alive, but also able to say that I have courage."
>
> —Helen Thayer, *Polar Dream*

"So I climbed down to Camp V and spent some of the most exhausting, painful hours of my life. I kept thinking, 'What if those climbers die because I couldn't get to them?' I busied myself with melting snow for water. Finally, I saw the climbers in the distance, walking toward camp. Everything was fine, and the water was very much needed for them to rehydrate. My decision to turn around had been really difficult to make, but it turned out to be the right one and I learned a lot from it. It still gets to me at times. For a couple years, a little voice inside would say, 'You failed, you failed.'"

Heather added, "Now, when I'm on a mountain and faced with an obstacle, I remind myself, 'The universe is not going to give me something I can't handle and, for some reason, I need this experience to grow in whatever way I need to grow.'"

IDENTIFYING YOUR GOALS AND LEARNING STYLE

Before you run to the nearest mountaineering shop and start buying equipment, it is useful to ask yourself why you want to take up mountaineering. Do you have one special mountain that you've always wanted to climb? Are you interested in trying out a new sport? Do you have friends who head out to the mountains and you'd like to join them? Are you a backpacker, rock climber, or ice climber who would like to expand your range in the mountains? Are you a novice to outdoor adventure with a yearning to journey to high places?

The next step is to assess how you can safely take up this new sport. There may be a school or a professional guide service

> "**T**he goal is to appropriately challenge yourself, not get into a situation that is too much of a challenge. This is why it's good to start with a qualified person who has a thorough knowledge of your experience and can determine if this challenge is appropriate for you."
>
> —Barbara Harris

nearby that teaches mountaineering skills. Or perhaps you can join a mountaineering club that offers training. If you are fortunate enough, you may have a competent and trusted friend who can help you develop technique and judgment.

It is also important for you to assess your learning style. Do you learn most easily by simply engaging in the sport (and learning from your mistakes)? Do you like to back up firsthand experience with reading to clarify and expand your knowledge? Do you prefer to have a woman guide or to learn in a group that has other women? If these last two elements are important to you, be sure to inquire about them when you are investigating schools, guide services, and clubs.

If you decide to take instruction (or even if you're going with a skilled friend), ask lots of questions. Most guides and instructors have been climbing since their teens and have a lot of experience—and lots of "war stories"—to share.

Chapter 10, Resources, is a listing of mountaineering schools and books that might be of assistance as you begin your search for instruction.

Chapter 2

GETTING STARTED

When I asked Francey Blaugrund of Oakhurst, California, and Terry Austin of Ojai, California, to become the "volunteer" novice mountaineers for this book, they hesitated at first. Both worked for the U.S. Forest Service and were familiar with wilderness. Both were seasoned backpackers. But Francey had a fear of heights and Terry had never been on high wilderness terrain without her husband, Greg.

Francey's fear of heights was somewhat selective. She had no problem climbing onto the roof of her house or flying in a helicopter to backcountry fires, but stand her on the edge of an exposed ridge with the world seemingly falling away beneath her, and she'd freeze (as would a healthy number of people). To Francey, climbing Mount Rainier meant lots of exposed ridges.

"I would be venturing into the unknown," Francey added. "I was unsure how I would respond to the various challenges."

Terry and Greg backpacked together in the high Sierra Nevada mountains nearly every summer. Terry was accustomed to carrying a heavy backpack on rugged mountain trails, but had never climbed on glaciated terrain. Terry wasn't certain she'd be "good enough" to climb Rainier.

I understood Francey and Terry's feelings, as I'd had many of the same fears and anxieties when first starting out. But climbing has helped me overcome many of them (I still have trouble negotiating tall ladders). "You'll be shown how to use the proper gear and you'll be taught proper

MOUNTAIN WEATHER
• • • • • • • • • • • • • • • • •

Most mountaineers develop a healthy respect for weather. Despite your best efforts and excellent preparation, bad weather can be the single factor that prevents you from attaining your goal—the next camp, the summit, or the safety of your tent on the descent.

Learn to predict mountain weather. Study books and ask your guides questions about how to spot indicators of changing weather. Survival often depends on your ability to identify trends in weather. A quick drop in temperature or a sudden warming after heavy snowfall, a plume of snow blowing off a distant ridge or the summit, clouds rapidly converging on the mountain, the sky turning a hazy white—all are signs of impending change.

It's extremely dangerous to keep moving up a mountain in the face of bad weather, especially during high wind, heavy snowfall, or blizzard conditions. If your route becomes obliterated and your vision impaired, you become lost—which is big trouble in mountaineering. At the first sign

(continued on page 21)

climbing technique," I told them. "You'll be roped together in teams while on the glacier, and you'll be wearing crampons and carrying an ice axe. The emphasis will be on safety."

I related how climbing had helped me overcome more than just the fear of heights (except for the ladder thing; I'm still working on that). Mountain climbing teaches you to pace yourself, to focus on advancing one step at a time, to step and breathe in rhythm, to take periodic rest breaks to rehydrate and nourish your body, to advance up the mountain slowly but steadily, to work as part of a rope team, and to exhibit patience for a slow climber ahead of or behind you—or to appreciate another's patience when that slow climber is you. These experiences translate into real-life lessons, such as learning to approach problem-solving with a "one step at a time" attitude and learning to pace yourself throughout a day, focusing on the task at hand instead of rushing ahead and allowing a multitude of "what-ifs" to impede your progress.

Another valuable lesson is patience—the saga of the tortoise and the hare is revisited on Mount Rainier! During a climb, Pete Whittaker, co-owner of RMI, reminds his clients to "Take it slow and easy, breathe and step, breathe and step. You see these other climbing parties rushing for the summit, taking lots of quick steps, then bending over to wheeze and catch their breath? We're pacing ourselves. Sooner or later we'll catch up to them and pass them because we're patient. The summit isn't going anywhere." The "one step at a time" philosophy I learned on the mountain also has been good for me off the mountain. I have a tendency to go at tasks like I'm killing snakes, and I have to remind myself to slow down, breathe, take it one step at a time.

Knowing that they would be the subject of a book also placed some performance anxiety on both Francey and Terry. "What if one of us or both of us don't make it to the top?" Terry asked.

"Whatever happens will be part of the experience," I said. "The weather might keep you from going to the summit, so try not to worry."

Ultimately, both Francey and Terry decided to go for it. "I decided to climb because I thought it would be good to step outside my comfort zone and do something totally new," said Francey. "I thought that mountain climbing might help me feel more at ease about stepping out of my routine and trying new experiences."

As for exposed ridges, she chose "not to think about that until it happens."

Terry decided that the climb would be an opportunity to "do something I never thought I could do, without Greg along to take care of me. I wanted to see if I really could do it," she said, "a mountain adventure under my own power, to test my strength—both physical and mental."

Francey and Terry's concerns were valid. Although experienced backpackers, they knew that there is a big difference between backpacking and mountain climbing, even though the latter incorporates many techniques of the former.

I first attempted to climb Mount Rainier in 1988, when I was 40. Always active, I enjoyed hiking, backpacking, and skiing. I lived in the foothills of the Sierra Nevada Mountains. To prepare for the climb, I carried a pack up and down a hill near my house, three times a week, for a couple of months.

By the time I arrived at Paradise, the base of Mount Rainier and location of the headquarters for the RMI guide service, I thought I was ready. I had a large backpack full of *everything* I thought I would need for five days on the mountain. Because I wanted to capture every moment, I also had a full 35-mm camera outfit with me, including separate telephoto and wide-angle lenses. Even though RMI was providing food, I had extra. I had packed more clothes than the gear list recommended. And when I strapped the ice axe and crampons onto the outside of my pack, I realized I had too much. I could hardly pick up the pack to get it on my back. The guides suggested that I lighten my load a little, by leaving some extras behind, but I wasn't about to leave any of my "necessities." So I struggled into the pack and off I went with our group.

The early June day had dawned bright, clear, and hot. We slogged for about an hour under 80-degree temperatures, caused by the full sun bouncing off snow. Luckily, I had followed the lead of our guides and other group members and worn shorts and a cotton T-shirt. But I also had on a polypropylene T-shirt under the cotton one (another extra!), thinking that I'd stay drier that way.

MOUNTAIN WEATHER

• • • • • • • • • • • • • • • •

(continued from page 20)
of bad weather, turn back to the safety of your previous camp, or make camp where you are, if possible. Don't move on until the storm is clearly over. You may even have to abandon the climb. But don't worry—the mountain will be there when you return. By playing it safe, you'll be alive to try the climb again under better conditions.

Climbers on Mount Rainier. (Keith Gunnar)

"**A**ccumulating technical skills as offered by guiding companies in the United States is very important. I wish I'd had that. There is something to be said about learning with a friend or partner, because you develop a lot of confidence quickly. But I remember going back and buying a book on knots, because I was improvising all the time. To the beginner I'd say, 'Take a class but also network beyond the class. Find partners. Gain proficiency through winter camping, extended backpacking trips, and rock climbing.'"

—Heidi Howkins, professional climber

During the first hour of what was to be a five- to six-hour hike to our base camp at Camp Muir at 10,000 feet, the sweat poured off me, wicked through the polypropylene, and absorbed into the cotton. When we stopped for a rest break, I gulped water and pulled off the polypropylene T-shirt, leaving the wet cotton T-shirt on my skin. That felt good until a breeze picked up and turned the pleasant cooling effect of the wet T-shirt into a freezing effect. (Later, I realized I should have removed the cotton T-shirt and worn the polypropylene.)

The terrain grew steeper as we headed for Pebble Creek, the second rest stop on the snowfield, where a creek is formed by melting snow off the glacier above. I was the last person to reach the rest break. Along the way, I had stopped sweating under my heavy load and now was just building up heat . . . and dizziness. The last thing I ever expected to be on this climb was hot. I didn't think to say anything to anyone until I stumbled into the Pebble Creek rest-break area around 7,800 feet and announced that I felt "woozy."

One of the guides came over to me and said, "You're going pretty slowly now. I don't think you've been drinking enough water and the load you're carrying is pretty heavy. It's about four hours more to Camp Muir. We could take some of your stuff and divide it up among the guides to carry. What do you think?"

"I think I'll see you next year." This climb was over for me. If I couldn't do it under my own steam, I wasn't going to do it. He sent me down with another guide.

I forced myself to remain cheerful during the comparatively easy hike *downhill* to Paradise, but inside I burned with embarrassment and shame. Why hadn't I trained harder? Why hadn't I listened to the guides? Why hadn't I trimmed down the contents of my pack, bought a point-and-shoot camera, and on and on until I grew tired of beating myself.

By the time I returned home, I had decided that I would begin training for another climb the following summer. I joined a gym for weight training. I trimmed down my pack and talked my mother into buying me a point-and-shoot camera for my birthday. The following June, off I went again. This time, I climbed with a lighter pack to Camp Muir. I wore shorts and a T-shirt made of synthetic fabric that dried quickly and didn't cling to my skin. On the mountain, I spent two days with my climbing group learning technique, from glacier walking and rope travel to ice climbing and rappelling. On the fourth day, the day of the summit attempt, the guides roused us at 1:30 in the morning. By 3 o'clock, guided by our headlamps shining on the snow, we were climbing. At the 12,300-foot rest break above a rocky abutment called Disappointment Cleaver, I decided to turn around. My legs had begun cramping and I was slowing down my rope team's progress. The guide left it up to me: "You can go on, but remember that you have to be able to go all the way back down, too." I had no idea of what was ahead of me, so I decided to turn back.

Two other women in the group turned back with me. One was an extremely fit and strapping 6-foot-tall Olympic-hopeful cyclist, the other was of average constitution and ran a bookstore. When we arrived back at Camp Muir, the cyclist admitted that she hadn't been eating since our

• •

"In 1980, I was doing business with Skip Yowell and Murray Pletz, the founders of JanSport, and they talked me into climbing Mount Rainier. I was 37, it sounded fun. I envisioned myself as Heidi with pigtails and goats. When I received a gear list from Skip—ice axe, backpack, sleeping bag, and so on—I called him and asked, 'Who carries these backpacks for us?' I had never heard of an ice axe. I thought it was something you used in a martini.

"I went. I was still smoking then. But I played tennis and skied, and felt like I shouldn't have a problem climbing. The first day, a blizzard prevented us from even hiking to Camp Muir base camp. We hiked as far as Pebble Creek, about 7,800 feet. I pulled a groin muscle and had to quit the climb.

"I signed up to climb the following year, and this time I worked out hard for it and I reached the summit. I rank that experience right up there with childbirth— incredibly joyous, an enormous physical effort requiring lots of tenacity. I went back to the mountain many more times, summited again, just to enjoy the mountain experience.

"I love the dynamics of the people on your rope, how a person's character comes out when he or she is faced with a mental or physical struggle. To be mentally capable of the endeavor of climbing a mountain is an incredible feeling. To take all your mental and physical strength to your known limit and then push a bit farther—you learn so much about yourself."

—Amber M. Brookman, CEO, Brookwood Companies

• •

group had arrived at Camp Muir four days before. She had never acclimatized to being at 10,000 feet and felt continually nauseated.

"Why didn't you tell anyone?" I asked, remembering my experience the year before.

She shrugged. "I guess I thought I'd get better every day. I don't understand. My body has never let me down." She was extremely depressed—not to mention weak—and climbed into her sleeping bag, refusing to discuss the topic further.

The other woman said that she had "hit the wall" at 12,300 feet and knew she had to turn back. Later, she confessed to me, "I could have gone on. But I had to poop and I couldn't bring myself to do it out there in front of everyone."

Talk about learning opportunities! I had to ask myself, what would I do in the same situations? Relieving myself in an exposed place was not a problem. After years of camping and backpacking, I knew that nobody wanted to watch anyway. Everyone either walks away or turns the other way while you perform your duty. But many people, and especially women, are modest about relieving themselves outdoors. During a climb of Argentina's 22,841-foot Aconcagua in 1995, one of the women on our team did not defecate for three days during the trek to base camp. We dug a rock pit at base camp, built a rock wall around it for privacy, *et voilà*! She triumphantly announced to the team, "The view from the privy beats the hell out of any magazine!"

Feeling too ill to eat or drink is a real problem for a mountain climber. The human body just won't go very far on empty. You can push yourself much farther at sea level. The higher you go, the more the atmospheric pressure decreases (e.g., around sea level, the barometric pressure is about 30 inches; on top of Everest, it's about 9 inches), and your body's craving for oxygen increases. The combination of decreased atmospheric pressure and oxygen deprivation causes your body's metabolism to work overtime. Calories burn like gasoline; in effect, your body begins to feed on itself.

Food and water not only fuel the climber's body, but also help fend off altitude sickness. Heather MacDonald tells her clients, "There are six ways to climb a mountain: eat, eat, eat, and drink, drink, drink."

At high altitude, 18,000 feet and above, ideally you need to feed your body 8,000 calories a day. This is difficult, because a common side effect of altitude is loss of appetite. But as Heather says, "You do the

"Mountaineering has become the most fulfilling experience in my life. I understand the lessons on a visceral level more than intellectually. The experience engages me and teaches me in a most condensed and compressed way.

"And the lessons are so simple! If you're cold, put on a jacket. If you're thirsty, drink water. Hungry, eat. Pay attention and adjust accordingly. It's a wise thing to learn. In adapting and pushing yourself through uncomfortable experiences, you learn to deal with the curveballs of everyday life."

—Barbara Harris

• •

"**C**ommon to many of the hundreds of accounts of women climbers I have read is
their honesty and their willingness to share personal emotion. For it is the psychological rather than the physical journey up the mountain that is of value to
the reader. When we see pictures of down-clad figures laboring up an icy
Himalayan peak or rock climbers in Lycra scaling steep crags, we often wonder
why people climb. And when the climbers are women—supposed to be the life-
giving rather than the life-risking sex—we are even more intrigued. Why would
a woman choose to challenge gravity, rock, and ice to climb a mountain? What
led her to these steep and dangerous places? How does she integrate this sport
into her personal and professional life?"

—Arlene Blum, from her preface to *Leading Out: Women Climbers Reaching for the Top*

• •

best you can." Eat, eat, eat, drink, drink, drink. Most climbers carry hard candy, candy bars, or
energy bars in their pockets for quick snacks and eat carbo-loaded meals in camp.

In the years since my first climb on Mount Rainier, I've noticed that I do not experience any
decrease in appetite until I'm over 14,000 feet. At sea level, I'm a chocoholic; on the mountain,
my craving for chocolate disappears. The irony is cruel!

On the same climb of Aconcagua in 1995, one of my tentmates never lost her appetite,
whether at 14,000, 16,000, or 19,000 feet. She'd gobble down her meals and ask for more. If you
had food left over in your bowl, she'd gladly finish it. At 46, she was strong, fit, and motivated. At
sea level, she monitored her diet, which was predominantly vegetarian, and denied herself chocolate. On the mountain, she'd eat anything, knowing that she'd burn it all off.

After my first attempt on Mount Rainier in 1988, I spent some time researching the cause
of my leg cramps and came to the conclusion that it was more than extreme exertion or tension in
the muscle. I tend to perspire heavily. Heavy perspiration can cause dehydration and loss of body
salt, leading to cramping. I've been advised to take a couple of salt tablets before heading for the
summit. You have to drink more water if you take salt tablets, but they can help prevent cramping.

I also reevaluated my training regimen. In climbing to 12,300 feet on Rainier, it became
painfully obvious that switchbacking up a steep slope—as one tends to do when backpacking—
isn't always feasible in mountaineering. Often, the terrain isn't even wide enough or safe enough
for switchbacking. The route leads straight up, one step after the other. Sometimes the lead
climber will *kick steps*, which involves kicking the toe of one's boot into the snow to make a platform for the next climber, who does the same kicking motion to make the step even more pro-
nounced for the next climber, and so on. On extremely steep terrain, climbers will sometimes use
their ice axes to chop out "buckets" in the wall to step into. To me, steep terrain is like walking

"Here I was . . . a 40-year-old woman who should have been dead from my addictions, but instead I was living in a tent, wearing wet socks and boots, and climbing over barren rocks on my way to the highest point on the African continent. One step at a time was how I learned to make it through a day in treatment. The same simple principles worked as well on this mountain as on the ones I was climbing inside. Show up, put one foot in front of the other, and extraordinary things can happen."

—Margo Chisholm, *To the Summit*

up a staircase—so I changed my workout routine to include stair climbing.

A word about stair-climbing machines, as commonly found at gyms today. I think they are useful for warming up for a workout, but I do not believe that they approximate the motion of climbing. When climbing, first you place one foot on a stable platform (snow, ice, or rock) and then you use your leg muscles to lift your body up to the next step. On a stair climber, one foot pushes a platform down (the pedal) while the other foot rises with the other platform. I find that my legs get a much better and more applicable workout for climbing by hiking steps, such as staircases or school bleachers, while wearing a loaded backpack. (This is discussed further in Chapter 3.)

Armed with all this new knowledge and a better workout regimen, I again set my sights on Mount Rainier. On two subsequent climbs, I felt strong and able. My legs didn't cramp as much, but when they did, I breathed harder and drank more water at the rest break. One time, I tried salt tablets; the next time, I went without. I learned that at altitude our bodies build up carbon dioxide and the main way that we get rid of it is through urinating. So staying hydrated helps the body acclimatize, and excess salt can get in the way of this process.

Drinking lots of water and breathing hard has helped me the most. (The technique for "breathing hard," also called *pressure-breathing,* is explained in Chapter 5.) I also got into the habit of drinking a quart of water before starting to climb each day, just to build my reservoir. Even so, on my third and fourth attempts on Rainier, high winds and ground blizzards prevented my party from reaching the summit. Each time, though, I learned something more about myself, my mental preparation, clothing systems, packing my pack, selecting gear, and learning technique. By the time I finally hit a stretch of good weather in July of 1995, I summited with ease.

Not everyone will go through such a prolonged "learning experience." Some people reach the summit their first time out. Some who are turned away never come back to try again. And some reach the summit and decide that mountaineering isn't for them and never return. There are many reasons to climb mountains, and just as many reasons not to. How can you be sure if you haven't ventured high? I don't know if the two women who turned back with me on my second Rainier climb ever tried again, but I hope they did.

Chapter 3

Ultimately, climbing Mount Rainier or any mountain requires strength and endurance. The RMI guides can relate many stories of fit people who had to turn back after hiking two hours, usually because they weren't used to carrying weight on their back uphill.

I shared my climbing experiences on Mount Rainier with Francey and Terry, and encouraged both to develop a workout routine that would fit their lifestyle.

"Continue whatever workout or activities you normally do, but add carrying a pack up and down stairs," I said. "If there are no stairs nearby, I recommend stepping up and down off a 12-inch stool or porch step, alternating legs. Carrying a loaded pack is one of the most important exercises you can do to prepare for a mountain climb."

A combination of endurance and aerobic conditioning is the best preparation. My mountain-climbing workout includes walking, hiking, a weight workout, and stair climbing for three to six months preceding a climb. If you've been inactive or are out of shape, I'd suggest starting at least six months before the climb. Here is my routine:

- Every morning, race-walk hills for about one hour; three times a week, carry a loaded backpack (for me, a pack weighing 30 to 35 pounds).

- Wear hiking boots for ankle support when carrying a pack; otherwise, running or walking shoes.

- Three times a week, do a 45-minute weight routine at the gym, including both free weights and universal machines. Focus on all parts of the body, with extra emphasis on legs (i.e., leg-press machine, lunges, squats).

- Three times a week, carry a loaded pack and walk up and down bleachers or stairs, or perform a step-up/step-down routine off a porch step, for about a half-hour.
  NOTE: Whenever you work out with your pack, concentrate on keeping your pace slow but steady. Focus on building endurance, not speed.

- Once or twice a week, take a half-day or all-day hike in the hills wearing a pack to simulate the endurance challenge of a climb. Several all-day hikes before you leave for your climb are even better—a typical "summit day" can last 10 to 14 hours.
  NOTE: Start out with a 20-pound pack and work up to at least 35 pounds or, at the most, a pack weighing equal to one-third of your body weight.

Although your legs do a lot of the work in carrying loads up a mountain, it's important to also develop upper-body strength for a general level of fitness. Upper-body strength will also help you hoist your pack and use your ice axe, rope, and other techniques that require arm and back muscles. If you don't belong to a gym, buy some hand weights or dumbells and do shoulder, back, and arm exercises. Do push-ups and pull-ups. Do not wear ankle weights while hiking because they can throw off your center of gravity and cause back or hip pain. Wear regular hiking boots instead. To prevent stationary repetitive workout routines from becoming extremely boring, listen to music! When doing porch-stepping, I always set a kitchen timer to ensure that I don't quit early.

Don't run yourself into the ground the first time out. Stretch your body before and after workouts. Start with a light pack and work up to a full one. Begin with light weights and work up to heavier weights (consult the trainer at your gym). Alternate hard and light training days. Increase initial short walks and hikes into longer outings. On occasion, push yourself to the limit and then beyond, but always listen to your body. If you hurt, stop or at least slow down. If you need a rest day, take it. Increase the elements of your routine—distance, weight—one at a time. If you start a workout routine several months in advance, you'll gradually build your level of fitness and more likely avoid injury.

During the Mount Rainier seminar, Francey and Terry's backpacks weighed between 40 and 45 pounds. They did not have to carry food, cooking utensils, stoves, fuel, or tents because RMI maintains a cook shack and bunkhouse at Camp Muir.

There are other expedition and winter-climbing seminars available to introduce you to carrying heavier loads and making camp on a glacier, melting snow for drinking water, and cooking at altitude in sub-zero weather. (See Chapter 10, Resources, for a listing of seminars.) During the five-day introductory seminar, the emphasis is on learning mountaineering technique.

In Chapter 4, I talk more about what type of gear and clothing comprise the weight in your pack. Here, I concentrate on how much weight to carry while working out. Backpacking guidelines state that a person should carry no more than one-quarter to one-third of his or her body weight. There are exceptions, depending on your level of fitness. Thirty-something RMI senior guide Catie Casson weighs a little more than a 100 pounds and regularly carries 50- and 60-pound loads up the mountain. Thirty-year-old mountaineer Heidi Howkins is 5-foot-3, weighs around 115 pounds, and works out with a 60-pound pack.

> "I weight train with the heaviest weights I can for endurance. For my legs, I use a higher repetition format with the thought in mind that I take more than ten steps up a mountain at a time. I work out my upper body, too, but not with high repetition. The legs are what power you."
>
> —Barbara Harris

"When trekking in (to base camp)," Heidi explains, "I usually carry the same weight as the porters, between 55 and 60 pounds. As we begin to carry loads from base camp to the higher camps, I'll start out with about 15 pounds. As I become acclimatized, I'll work up to about 50 or 55 pounds. On the summit bid itself, I carry emergency bivy supplies and a summit pack. Above 7,500 meters (24,600 feet), I can't carry more than 10 to 15 pounds."

To most people, 45 pounds doesn't sound heavy until they put it on their back and start hiking uphill. The U.S. Army conducted a study that revealed that 1 pound of weight carried on a person's back (in this case, a GI's back) translates to an extra 5 pounds of weight-bearing on the feet. A 45-pound pack, therefore, puts an additional 225 pounds of pressure on your feet, in addition to your own body weight. This is why it's wise to begin working out with a light pack, especially if carrying a backpack is a new experience.

If you are not accustomed to carrying a pack, start with a load of 10 or 15 pounds, until you feel comfortable carrying that weight. (Load your pack with actual gear or use weights, pillows, or kitty litter. Put the pack on and step on a scale to determine the weight.) Use the same backpack you plan to carry on the climb (selecting packs is discussed in Chapter 4). Add 5 pounds each week until you reach 30 pounds. During this time, you'll also be increasing the length of your hikes and the time spent working out. Remain at 30 pounds for two or three weeks, then increase to 40 or 45 pounds for the last three to four weeks before you leave for your mountaineering destination.

If you are accustomed to carrying a backpack while hiking or rock climbing, and you are already fit, start with more weight, such as 20 or 25 pounds. After one week, increase the weight to 30 or 35; in two weeks, go to 40 or 45 pounds.

Both Terry and Francey work demanding, full-time schedules. Each adapted her own work-

FITNESS IS PHYSICAL AND MENTAL

••••••••••••••••••

Mountaineer Heidi Howkins concentrates on building strength and flexibility—both physical and mental—to train for a climb. "Often, I put on a 60-pound backpack and go flat out on the Stairmaster for 10 minutes. I also do a lot of slow long-distance runs—if possible, in hills for two to four hours each time." She adds, "During a workout, it's good to learn to push yourself. It takes a lot of mental devotion to push your body without missing messages, without playing mental games with yourself—and that's also part of the training, pushing beyond the physical limits you set for yourself.

(continued on page 31)

out routine. Terry rode her bike to work three days a week, 45 minutes each way. Luckily, there is a workout room at her office, making it convenient for her to go in early and spend about 15 minutes a day doing upper-body weight training, two or three sets of 12 reps each. When she was working in the field, she added weight to the pack she carries at work to take advantage of the opportunity to train. In addition, twice a week, she put on the pack she planned to carry on Rainier and hiked up a training trail used by the fire-engine crew to maintain fitness. "The trail goes just about straight up," she told me. "It takes me 30 minutes to go up and about 25 to come down [she descended slowly to protect her knees]. I started with a 20-pound pack and in three weeks increased it to 30 pounds." On weekends, Terry rode her mountain bike a couple of hours a day, took a two- to four-hour hike with her husband and their two dogs, or hiked the stadium steps at the local college with her 40-pound pack.

In her work in reforestation, Francey walks hills all day long. She supplemented this convenient workout with the porch-step routine three or four times a week. Each day after work, she also alternated running for an hour in the afternoon with carrying her 35-pound pack up and down the local high-school bleachers.

Left: Terry working out in the mountains. (Greg Austin) **Above:** Francey working out on high school bleachers.

"**W**hen you are physically fit for climbing a mountain, you know something that others don't. That is, ordinary fitness is not enough to do extraordinary things. You have to be extraordinarily fit to do extraordinary things."

—Amber M. Brookman

FITNESS IS PHYSICAL AND MENTAL

(continued from page 30)
The mental part is the most important part of a climb. Some climbs are 90 percent mental. If you can stay relaxed and comfortable in the medium, you'll move with more efficiency.

"After a workout," she says, "I love to go in the sauna and meditate or do isometrics or sit-ups. For relaxation training, I swim, leisurely, without tension."

Professional guide and mountaineer Heather MacDonald climbs mountains for a living. For relaxation, and cross training, she flamenco dances.

On weekends, she took her pack to the local mountains and hiked about four hours at 6,000-foot elevation.

Realistically, you might not be able to work out two hours a day. Whatever you do, be sure to do these things: Two or three times a week, run or race-walk to build aerobic capacity; three times a week, carry a pack up and down bleacher steps or staircases to build strength (this also provides a good aerobic workout); twice a week, do total body weight training; and once a week (such as on the weekend), take one long hike with your loaded pack to build endurance.

During your workouts, be sure to drink plenty of water to get in the habit of staying hydrated.

On the mountain, dehydration will bring on a splitting headache, possibly nausea, indigestion, and cramping. During a recent climb of 19,340-foot Mount Kilimanjaro in Africa, one of the members of my party began to complain about a headache. I asked her if she was drinking lots of water. She shook her head and said, "I don't like water." Nothing anyone said, including our guides, could convince her that her increasing malaise was due primarily to dehydration. Needless to say, she became too ill to ascend to the summit.

People have successfully climbed Mount Rainier with little preparation. On one of my climbs, there was a woman who had trained by carrying a loaded pack "about three times" the week before she left for the mountain. She regularly attended aerobic-dancing classes and she looked pretty healthy. She made it to the summit, although—as she told me afterwards—"the guide all but pulled me to the top. When we got up there, it was cloudy and I couldn't see anything. I said to the guide, 'This is *it?*'" She later commented, "It was the hardest thing I've ever done. I hurt all the way. I will never do it again."

When I asked her why she even came to Mount Rainier in the first place, she replied, "At the last minute, my boss couldn't go and asked me if I wanted to go in his place. I said, 'Sure.'"

I can't say that her experience was a waste of time. In fact, I'd be willing to bet that she still thinks about struggling arm in arm with her guide to the summit. Deep down inside, she might even entertain the thought of going back some day and climbing the mountain under her own power.

My advice is to be in the best shape you can be to make the adventure worthwhile.

Chapter 4

EQUIPMENT

The pursuit of high summits involves climbing on a variety of terrain, including long approaches over dusty, rocky terrain; slogging up soft, sloping snowfields; crossing crevasse-creased glaciers; and scaling steep ice and sharp rock outcrops. Temperatures range from sub-zero to blistering hot. Big mountains attract big storms. High winds, blowing snow, rain, and sleet are normal occurrences. For these reasons, the mountaineering gear and clothing list is somewhat extensive and expensive. But once you've made the initial investment, there are no lift tickets or lodges, dock or launching fees to hinder your progress.

While you're getting started, consider renting certain pieces of gear from your local outdoor or mountaineering shop. Plastic mountaineering boots, crampons, ice axes, helmets, harnesses, backpacks, and sleeping bags are common rental items. When you're ready to invest in your own gear, remember that manufacturers of quality gear usually offer a lifetime warranty. Therefore, buy the best that you can afford—it will last longer and perform better.

Here's my recommended and annotated list for a five-day Mount Rainier climb. Note that most guide services supply food, stove, cooking utensils, and tents. The appendix is a concise list of all gear, clothing, and optional items described in this chapter.

CLOTHING

The goal is to create a layering system of clothing that enables you to adjust to changing temperatures. For the five-day Mount Rainier climbing seminar, you'll need five layers for the upper body, three layers for the lower body.

As you exert, your body generates heat and perspiration. The correct layering system of garments made from synthetic fabrics will move the excess heat and moisture vapor away from your skin to the outside of the clothing ensemble for evaporation and quick drying. This will help you maintain a comfortable body temperature.

When you're in an outdoor store shopping for performance clothing, you'll hear terminology such as *breathability*, *wicking*, and *moisture management*. Breathability refers to how well a fabric allows moisture vapor to pass through its construction. Breathability is often used in conjunction with *waterproof*, as in *waterproof/breathable*, which describes a garment that is engineered to repel rain while allowing moisture vapor inside to escape to the outside (instead of clammily condensing against your skin). As long as the temperature outside the garment is colder than the temperature inside, this breathability process works. Mechanical ventilation systems (e.g., armpit zippers and chest vents) enhance this process, especially on balmy days. Wicking refers to a fabric's ability to absorb and spread moisture throughout a given area for more rapid evaporation. Moisture management describes the fabric's action of pushing and pulling moisture from the inside (near the body) to the outside. The result of all this activity is a drier, more comfortable garment that will protect you from hypothermia as well as the elements.

Everyone loves cotton—it's the comfort fabric of choice for most Americans. But it's the bane of mountaineers. I've heard this succinct way of describing the attributes of cotton: "Cotton kills." Cotton T-shirts are fine when you're not climbing, or when you're on the lower part of the mountain on a warm sunny day. However, in a layering system, cotton will remain wet, suck the heat from your body, and become a deadly contributor to hypothermia. So, avoid cotton for layering on the mountain.

Let's start from the outside and work our way in.

- **Hooded down parka.** Except on extremely cold or high mountains, mountaineers rarely climb in down parkas. But at camp or rest breaks, a hooded down-insulated parka will become your new best friend, holding in precious body heat while you rehydrate and nourish yourself. For sleeping, the parka is also useful as an extra insulating layer. Look for 550 or higher *fill power* (the measure used to determine the warmth-to-weight ratio of down; fills are usually 550, 650, 700, or 750). A good alternative is a synthetic-insulated parka, such as one that uses Polarguard, Thinsulate, or Primaloft insulation. If down gets wet, it loses its insulating power; however, synthetic insulations will retain warmth when damp. The tradeoff is that most synthetic insulations are heavier and less compressible than down. When shopping, compare both and choose the one

insulated
windproof hat

glacier glasses

insulated, down-
filled parka

insulating
fleece jacket

waterproof, breathable
Gore-Tex® jacket
(non-insulated)

thermal
underwear

waterproof, breath-
able Gore-Tex® outer
mitten with insulating
pile mitten liner

waterproof
gaiters

non-insulated, waterproof
breathable Gore-Tex®
bibs with thermal under-
wear underneath

plastic mountaineering
boots with warm
socks

that fits your weight-carrying and warmth needs. Remember, the parka must be large enough to be zipped up when wearing up to four layers underneath (i.e., a non-insulated "shell" parka, fleece jacket, and two layers of thermal underwear).

- **Hooded weatherproof parka.** Look for windproof, breathable, waterproof, or highly water-resistant performance features. Jackets and parkas made of Gore-Tex® fabric are most popular and are offered by most outerwear manufacturers, including Marmot Mountain Ltd., The North Face, Sierra Designs, Mountain HardWear, Wild Roses, REI, and L.L. Bean. But there are other fabrics that will serve you well, including Lowe Alpine Systems' Triple Point Ceramic, Patagonia's H2NO Storm, and Helly-Hansen's Helly-Tech. These are designed to be durable, abrasion-resistant, and weatherproof in harsh conditions. Look for a two-way full front zipper that can be zipped up from the bottom and down from the top, as well as underarm or chest vents. Try on the parka with a backpack to make sure that the waistbelt does not cover the jacket pockets. The parka should not be longer than hip length or it will interfere with your harness (worn underneath). It also must be big enough to zip up over three layers (i.e., a fleece jacket and two layers of thermal underwear).

- **Full-side-zip, weatherproof pants or bibs.** Look for the same fabric as described previously. Full-side zippers make it easy to get pants or bibs on and off without having to remove boots. Bibs provide more coverage for the upper body than pants and usually have a convenient chest pocket (for carrying sunscreen, lip gloss, tissues, energy bars, candy), as well as suspenders that allow you to drop the seat of your pants to relieve yourself without also having to drop the front. This feature not only provides some privacy, but also helps maintain body heat if you have to relieve yourself during exceptionally chilly weather or a full-on blizzard. Many mountaineering pants also include "drop-seat" suspenders, and some newer styles of women's pants and bibs (e.g., from Marmot Mountain Ltd. and L.L. Bean) offer a split crotch or "pee system" that allows you to simply squat, pull apart (or unzip) the fabric, and go. Of course, your undergarments must have the same feature for this system to work properly. Pants or bibs must be large enough to wear over two layers (i.e., fleece pants and thermal underwear).

- **Fleece or pile jacket.** These are jackets made of the velour-like or nubby plush fabric you see everyone wearing on the street as well as in the outdoors. Made of synthetic fiber such as polyester or acrylic, the fabric is lightweight, quick-drying, and insulating when damp. It won't stretch out of shape, you can throw it in the washer and dryer when you get home from a two-week, "wore-it-everyday" marathon outing, and it comes out looking fresh. Some popular brands are Polartec, Synchilla, and GlenPile. I prefer a "technical" zip-up jacket with zippered pockets for more versatility, although many climbers like pullovers with long, ventilating front zippers.

Technical jackets also include underarm pit zippers and reinforcing nylon patches on shoulder and elbow. There are many weights of fleece and pile. For mountaineering, I recommend mid- or heavy-weight. Your outdoor specialty shop employee can tell the difference if the garment is not well marked.

(NOTE: Windproof fleece and pile garments have recently become very popular. I like this application in accessories such as vests, hats, and gloves; however, a full windproof fleece or pile jacket [or pant] can become too warm for some people. In general, women tend to get colder than men, so if you have a chance to try both windproof and regular, do so to find out which works best for you. Make certain the garment is large enough to wear over two layers of thermal underwear, onc lightweight and the other heavyweight.)

- **Fleece or pile pants or tights.** There are many styles available, from slim-fitting tights to pull-on "sweat-type" pants to full-side-zip technical pants with reinforcing nylon butt and knee patches. Some climbers like to climb in full-side-zip fleece pants rather than an outer shell. In a fall, fleece and pile hold better on snow and ice than nylon or polyester shells. As a well-known climber once remarked, "That nylon stuff is slicker than snot in an icy parking lot." Full-side-zip pants are highly recommended for easy adjustment of layering systems. Whatever style you choose, it should accommodate at least one layer of thermal underwear.

- **Lightweight synthetic thermal underwear top and bottom.** Cotton long johns, while comfortable to wear around the family cabin or to football games, are not appropriate for mountaineering, as discussed previously. Choose thermal underwear made of polypropylene, wool, or one of the many polyesters, such as Thermastat, Capilene, or Polartec. (I also like Coolmax for a lightweight layer.) There are a host of brands. Choose a lightweight top that fits as your "base layer." Styles of tops vary, from crewneck to turtleneck and mock-turtleneck or henley. Bottoms are usually straightforward: pull-on with elastic waist. If you like the "pee system" concept, look for the split-crotch style, such as those sold by Marmot and L.L. Bean. On a sunny day on the glacier, a lightweight top also doubles as additional sun protection.

- **Heavyweight synthetic thermal underwear top and bottom.** These come in the same fabrics as discussed previously, but in a heavier-weight knit construction for more warmth. I've found that a set each of lightweight and heavy-

FIT FOR WOMEN
• • • • • • • • • • • • • • • • • • • •

For years, women moun-
taineers have had to settle for
wearing men's clothing and
using men's gear. In some
instances and for some
women's body frames, this
works—but for most women,
it doesn't. In general, women
have narrower shoulders,
shorter overall body length,
shorter and slimmer arms, a
fuller chest but a smaller back.
Waists are narrower than
men's, but hips are fuller;
inseams are shorter, but the
rise is longer and more pro-
portioned.

We've all heard about
"unisex" clothing, supposedly
designed to fit both men and
women. Truly, there is no such
thing. Unisex is men's sizing. A
woman who normally wears a
women's size medium supposedly wears a unisex (or men's)
size small. But when a medium
woman wears a man's small
garment, she will swim in the
upper portion of the jacket
while the bottom will be snug.
The men's small pant will be
too long in the leg, big for her
waist, and tight through the
hip. It will be too long in the
front rise and too short in the
back rise.

(continued on page 39)

weight thermals work well for layering together or wearing alone. On summit day, I often start out wearing my heavyweight thermal top, shell jacket, and climbing bibs. I carry my lightweight thermal top, fleece jacket, and down parka in my pack, as the weather is sure to change sometime between dawn and dark. And, every time we stop for a rest and rehydration break, I pull on my insulated parka to preserve my body heat. The heavyweight pair of thermals should be large enough to be worn over a lightweight pair.

- **Sport bra and synthetic panties.** Cotton bras and panties will absorb perspiration and turn cold on you. Buy a synthetic-fabric sport bra and undies (my favorites are Moving Comfort's T3 mesh panties and Olympia bra, which includes a Coolmax liner); both will provide dry comfort.

- **Three pairs of wool socks.** I save a clean pair for summit day and alternate the other two on other days. Remember, no cotton or cotton blends! Helpful hint: On summit day, throw a dry "used" pair in your pack as a backup in case your gloves get blown into a crevasse.

- **Warm hat with ear coverage.** A wool or fleece/pile cap (windproof or not) with earflaps can be worn with or without your parka hood. On cold nights, the hat also will help retain body heat while you sleep.

- **Sun hat or ball cap.** Great for warm sunny days on the glacier, to protect from glare and sunburn.

- **Balaclava.** A *balaclava* is a knit hood that can be pulled down over the forehead and up over the nose to protect your face from stinging cold. When not in use, it can be pushed down and worn as a neck gaiter. A neoprene or fleece facemask such as those made by Seirus can be substituted.

- **Bandanna.** This is the only cotton item I carry in my pack. Good on hot days for wearing around the neck for sun protection, around the head to absorb sweat, or for wiping off sunscreen.

- **Shorts.** Take them along for approach hikes and climbing to Camp Muir on Mount Rainier on a hot day. If the weather looks forbidding, leave them in the car, as you won't use them on the upper mountain (above 10,000 feet). Lightweight nylon or polyester hiking shorts are best because they dry quickly and add less weight to your pack than cotton canvas shorts. Many climbers wear a lightweight thermal underwear top and bottom with a pair of shorts and a ball cap during the approach to base camp, then add layers if the wind comes up or the weather turns wet.

- **Waterproof shell gloves or mittens.** The layering system extends to your extremities too. Wear shell gloves or mittens over the other two glove layers in cold or windy situations to prevent frostbite. The shells must be waterproof and windproof. If your fingers get wet and then are exposed to freezing cold, frostbite is imminent.

- **Fleece or wool gloves or mittens.** Medium- to heavy-weight gloves or mittens comprise the middle of your glove-layering system. These can be worn alone or in combination with the shells and/or lightweight liners. Whether you choose gloves or mittens is up to you. Mittens tend to be warmer because you can curl up your fingers onto your own skin, but gloves provide more dexterity. If you have a chance to try both, do it. If you ski, you probably have already made a choice that best suits you.

FIT FOR WOMEN

(continued from page 38)

Although some women can wear shell garments that are sized for men, problems arise when they layer underneath those shells and discover that the extra fabric in the shoulders, sleeves, and legs becomes big, bulky, and restrictive instead of "fashionably oversized." Confine oversized garments to street wear, not to mountain-climbing attire!

For mountain climbing, clothing should be well fitted and allow unrestricted freedom of motion. Extra fabric will hinder movement and, in a pant, possibly obstruct your view of your feet when climbing or get caught on one of your crampon points and cause a fall.

Most major outerwear manufacturers now make women's performance clothing (among them, Arc'Teryx, Helly-Hansen, Lowe Alpine Systems, Marmot Mountain Ltd., Moonstone, Mountain HardWear, Patagonia, Sierra Designs, The North Face, and Wild Roses).

- **Lightweight glove liners.** A thin pair of synthetic-fabric gloves, such as polypropylene or Thermastat, are good for warm days on the glacier when you need protection from sun as well as from abrasive ice and snow. This is your next-to-skin layer when worn in combination with heavier mittens or gloves under a waterproof and windproof shell.

- **Waterproof gaiters.** Gaiters are worn over climbing boots and lower pants legs to enhance wind- and water-proofness and, therefore, keep your feet warmer. They must fit snugly over the top of your boot and extend up to just below the knee, such as the "Crocodiles" from Outdoor Research. The first time you *post-hole* (i.e., sink in to your knees in deep snow), you'll be glad you have them.

- **Plastic mountaineering boots.** Consisting of a plastic shell (not unlike a ski boot) plus a removable inner boot, these are designed for protection and stability. The stiff plastic, of course, is totally windproof and waterproof, and helps create a platform for climbing where there is little or none. The boots also help prevent ankle and lower-leg strain. Leather crampon-compatible mountaineering boots are making something of a comeback. Leather conforms better to the foot and offers more flexibility, but also will soften up over time and lose some support. Plastic boots remain stiff for the life of the boot. Most mountaineers do not recommend using leather boots above 19,000 feet or in extreme cold conditions. Novices should start out in plastic boots.

  In general, women's feet are narrower than men's, overall. With some exceptions, women with smaller feet (i.e., size 8 or smaller) tend to have narrow heels and wide forefeet; women with feet size 8½ or larger tend to have narrow forefeet. Therefore, most women have difficulty fitting their feet into men's boots. There are very few plastic mountaineering boots designed to the contours of a woman's foot (Koflach, Raichle, and Lowa offer ladies' models). If you can't find a woman's boot to rent or borrow, take time to try on several sizes and types of men's plastic boots to get the best fit you can.

  A plastic mountaineering boot should hold your heel snugly, but provide plenty of toe room. When trying on, be sure to wear the same socks you plan to wear on the mountain. (Heavy mountaineering socks, such as those from Smart Wool, and an extra insole, such as those made by Sorbothane or Spenco, often can take up the extra volume of a man's boot. You might also consider having a custom footbed built by SuperFeet, a service available at many ski and outdoor shops.) Wiggle your toes to test the forefoot volume. If possible, stand on a slanted surface to make certain that your toes don't cram into the front of the boot. During exertion, your feet will probably swell some. When coming down a mountain, gravity and your body weight drive your feet into the front of the boot. To prevent cramping and toe-bruising, make certain your toes have enough room to move. If the boot is too tight, it will restrict circulation and lead to pain and, in the extreme, frostbite. Go to a larger size, another model, or another brand until you find the best fit.

- **Down booties.** My only luxury item, I wear down booties in the hut at Camp Muir or in a tent. Make sure the bottoms are made of water-resistant Cordura nylon or coated nylon for waterproofness. Some climbers wear their inner boots around camp, but I like to keep mine as dry and warm as possible for climbing. Down booties are lightweight and easy to stuff into a nook in your backpack. Synthetic-insulated booties can be substituted for down.

GEAR

Everything discussed in this equipment chapter goes to Camp Muir, the 10,000-foot base camp on Mount Rainier, and some of it goes higher. And guess who gets to carry it? That's right, you. Pay attention to the weight of each item on the following list. Most technical gear and clothing is made to maximize performance while minimizing weight. Once you start buying gear, it's easy to go overboard because there's lots of neat stuff. To curb impulse buying, remind yourself that you have to carry all of it.

A basic mountaineering gear list contains just about the same number and type of items for a man as for a woman. Many of the items weigh the same or within an ounce or two of each other, including sleeping bag, ground pad, clothing, headlamp, crampons, and ice axe. At the least (without having to carry fuel, stove, food, and tent), your pack will weigh around 45 pounds. Fully outfitted for a tenting expedition on a glaciated mountain, the pack will weigh closer to 65 pounds, depending on how long you plan to be out. A 5-foot-4 woman who weighs 135 pounds is going to struggle with this weight a lot more than a 5-foot-10 male who weighs 165 pounds. Even so, it can be done if you are fit, have trained with a pack, know

Hiking poles, internal frame pack with ice axe, carabiners, water bottles, accessory cord, and mountaineering boots. Ready to go! (Francey Blaugrund)

how to stay hydrated, learn to pace yourself, and breathe properly while exerting.

- **Backpack.** There are two basic types of backpacks: internal frame and external frame. External frame packs are those with—you guessed it—an external frame.

The frame is usually made of aluminum, although some newer models incorporate graphite and plastic components. A large bag is attached to this frame. The bag has a couple of roomy compartments and several smaller pockets. Designed to carry a large load, the external frame pack gives its best performance on trails, where balance is not as crucial. For mountain climbing, many people prefer an internal frame pack. In this type of pack, the internal frame or structure is built to conform to the contours of the user's back. As a result, the pack rides closer to the body and is easier to balance on steep or uneven terrain. For mountain climbing, you'll need a pack with at least 5,500 cubic inches of carrying capacity.

Several companies now make backpacks designed to fit the contours of a woman's body. Many women need narrower shoulder straps to prevent them from digging into the side of their neck. Typically, women have a shorter torso length, so you'll find many packs with adjustability in this area. (In fact, this feature has been incorporated into some men's packs to accommodate shorter men.) A woman needs a hip or waist belt with more flare to it than a man's. And, because the space between a woman's ribs and hips is shorter than a man's, the waistbelt needs to be narrower. Beware of backpacks that tower over your head! Women have a lower center of gravity, so they need a pack that will allow them to carry the load somewhat lower. Be sure to buy your backpack from a specialty outdoor shop with experienced sales personnel who can show you how to adjust the right pack to your body. Some brands come with interchangeable waistbelts and shoulder harnesses to ensure a customized fit. Top brands to look for include Dana Design, Lowe Alpine Systems, Mountainsmith, Gregory, Osprey, The North Face, Arc'Teryx, Kelty, and JanSport.

- **Adjustable hiking poles.** Use these while carrying loads to and from base camp (you'll leave them there and use your ice axe on the upper mountain). Studies have shown that the use of hiking or trekking poles relieves your hip and knee joints of part of the load; they also provide balance and help you maintain a comfortable pace. Adjust them so your arms are bent at a right angle, going both uphill and downhill (you'll retract the length for uphill, extend it for downhill). Leki-U.S.A. and Life-Link both make adjustable hiking poles.

- **Sleeping bag.** If you plan to sleep inside the wooden hut at Camp Muir, a sleeping bag rated to provide warmth at 10 or 20 degrees will be sufficient. If you plan to sleep outside in a tent or snow cave, use a bag rated to zero degrees or warmer. A down-filled bag will be lighter than a similarly rated synthetic-insulated bag, but care must be taken not to get the down bag wet. Stuff it into a waterproof stuff sack lined with a plastic garbage bag for extra precaution.

In 1994, Sierra Designs introduced sleeping bags for women, based on the company's research that showed that women's body temperature is lower than men's during sleep. Sierra Designs beefed up the insulation, especially in the mid-section and foot of the bag, yet also contoured the bag for a woman's body—narrower in the shoulder, broader at the hip, and slimmer at the foot. The bags are shorter overall and designed to fit women up to either 5-foot-4 or 5-foot-10. (Taller women are encouraged to buy a standard sleeping bag.)

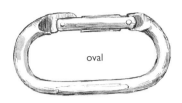

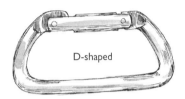

- **Ground pad.** A self-inflating mattress or foam pad adds a layer of cushioning and also insulates you from the cold ground (or bunk). When camping on snow, I like to use both an ensolite foam pad and a self-inflating Therm-a-Rest mattress.

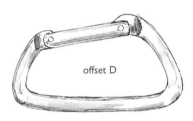

- **Three carabiners, two locking.** Carabiners are snap-link devices made of aluminum alloy, in many shapes and sizes. Climbers use them in a variety of ways, including to attach a climbing rope to a harness, to clip into safety anchors, for belaying, for rappelling, and for clipping gear to packs. The gate is the hinged part that opens; a locking carabiner has a sleeve that screws down over one end of the gate to prevent it from accidentally opening. Avoid "self-locking" carabiners, which can open by themselves all too easily.

- **Ice axe.** Never leave base camp without it! A versatile tool and a climber's best friend, the ice axe becomes a third point of balance on uneven or steep trails, a brake for going downhill or arresting a fall, a climbing tool, and an implement for digging in snow. With its pick, adze, and spike, it also can inflict wounds on the user or fellow climbers, so exercise caution in carrying and using it. (See Chapter 6 for proper ice-axe techniques.)

Six types of carabiners.

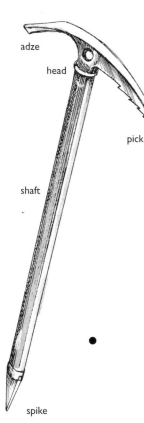

adze

head

pick

shaft

spike

Ice axe.

Ice axes vary in length, from approximately 40 to 90 centimeters (eighteen inches to 3 feet) long. For most mountaineering situations, including occasional ice climbing, use an ice axe of 55 to 70 centimeters, depending on your height. I am 5-foot-4 and use a 60-centimeter (about 2-foot) ice axe. When I hold the head of the axe, the spike or tip of the shaft doesn't quite reach the floor. For me, an axe much longer than 60 centimeters would be unwieldy for ice climbing situations. And shorter ice axes, while best for ice climbing, don't provide much leverage for self-arrest. Aluminum ice axes are preferred over wooden ones these days because they're lighter and stronger.

To keep from losing the ice axe, make a leash by cutting a length of cord or webbing about as long as the axe itself. Girth hitch one end to the head of the axe and tie an overhand knot in the other end, creating a loop to slide over your wrist. If done properly, the leash should be long enough to allow you to hold the axe at the end of its shaft, just above the spike.

Crampons. These consist of a steel frame with spikes for providing traction on snow and ice. Crampons attach to mountaineering boots with straps ("strap-on" style) or a combination of strap and wire bail ("step-in" style). RMI uses strap-on hinged crampons from Seattle Manufacturing Company.

Crampons have either a hinged or rigid construction. Hinged crampons are designed for general mountaineering on "mixed routes" of ice, snow, and rock. They flex at the instep, allowing for a natural walking motion, and can be attached to any type of mountaineering boot. When affixed to a boot with a stiff sole, such as a plastic mountaineering boot, hinged crampons are adequate for basic ice climbing. Rigid crampons, with a stiffness that provides more support during prolonged front-pointing (climbing on ice walls using only the front points of the crampon), are preferred for technical ice climbing. If used on flexible boots, rigid crampons can eventually fail from metal fatigue.

Both types of crampons are available in either strap-on or step-in configurations. Straps (preferably made of non-absorbent, non-stretching, non-rotting neoprene-coated nylon instead of leather) with buckles offer a very reliable method of attaching a crampon to a boot—whether plastic or leather. The ability to adjust the straps allows you to avoid cutting off circulation to your feet.

A step-in crampon binding commonly consists of a wire toe and heel bail (or heel lever). A strap to the ankle from the toe bail prevents you from losing the crampon should it come off the boot. Crampons with step-in bindings require an exact fit to the boot. The boot must have an adequate groove in the toe and heel specifically designed to accommodate the wire bail or heel lever.

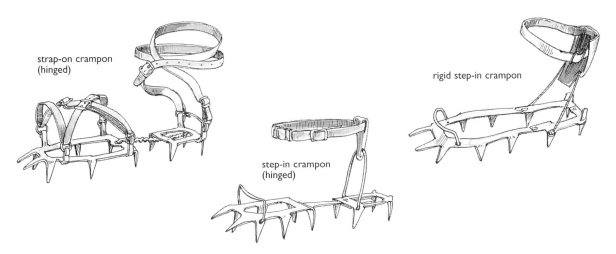

Three types of crampons: strap-on, step-in, and rigid step-in.

The versatility and easy fit of the strap-on crampon make it ideal for novice mountaineers as well as for those mountaineers using insulating overboots when climbing on extremely cold peaks, such as on Alaska's Mount McKinley or the Himalayas. An overboot will not accommodate step-in crampons.

- **Headlamp with extra batteries.** This is an indispensable tool that leaves your hands free to rummage in your pack, carry a rope and ice axe, melt snow, or cook a meal in the dark. Headlamps come with either built-in battery cases or separate battery packs that attach to a belt or clothing to protect battery life. Most summit attempts begin before dawn. Extreme cold will sap a set of exposed new AA batteries in an hour or less. Choose a headlamp with a separate battery pack or with a lithium or 4.5-volt battery so that you're not continually fumbling with the lamp and halting your group's progress in order to replace batteries. Many climbers favor the Petzl headlamp with 4.5-volt battery.

- **Glacier glasses with side shields.** These sunglasses come with darker lenses to shield your eyes from the extreme glare of sun bouncing off snow or ice. The leather or fabric "side shields" also protect from side glare, as well as blowing snow or ice debris. Some models have removable side shields so that the glasses also can be used for everyday wear. Most glacier glasses can be fitted with prescription lenses by a qualified optician. Popular brands include Bolle, Julbo, and Vuarnet.

- **Goggles.** In a blizzard, goggles will do a better job of protecting your eyes and are less likely to get blown off your head than sunglasses. There are goggles made to fit over glasses, for prescription-eyeglass wearers, such as those from Smith Sport Optics.

- **Two 32-oz. Lexan plastic water bottles.** Some climbers carry three bottles to ensure hydration. I drink a whole bottle of water before starting out in the morning, then replenish my two bottles with fresh snow or creek water along the way. A narrow-mouth bottle is easier to drink from, but a wide-mouth bottle allows you to easily pack snow into it for melting. Lexan plastic, such as used by Nalgene, doesn't crack in the cold. If you are climbing in areas where water quality is in question, treat your drinking water with iodine tablets (such as Potable Aqua) or use a purification filter (such as one from PŪR, SweetWater, MSR, Katadyn, or General Ecology).

    (NOTE about hydration packs: These are great for more temperate climates. A cold wind can freeze the water inside the drinking tube or bite valve and cut off your water supply. If you can find a hydration pack with a bag that opens wide enough to stuff snow inside and a tube and bite valve that are insulated against freezing, go ahead and bring it along; otherwise, stick to water bottles.)

- **Eating and cooking utensils.** For the Mount Rainier five-day climb, you will need only a bowl, spoon, and mug. For your own or other outings, you'll need a set of nesting pots and durable utensils. Try to eat everything out of one bowl instead of taking both a bowl and a plate. Your mug should be insulated with a snap-on cover for both hot and cold liquids.

- **Stove.** If you already have a backpacking stove, make sure it is made to function at high altitude and in cold climates. If you plan to climb in foreign countries, you will want a multi-fuel or kerosene stove because white gas is not readily available overseas.

- **Repair kit.** There are several on the market. Make sure yours includes short lengths of bailing wire and extra screws to repair crampons, and duct tape, which is handy for patching rips and tears.

ADDITIONAL GEAR

Every climber should carry self-extrication gear, including two prusiks (a length of cord with a knot that grips the rope when weighted, but moves easily when unweighted) or mechanical ascenders, a snow picket, a pulley, and at least three extra locking carabiners. The front and rear climbers on a rope should be carrying two snow pickets each. (Ropes are discussed in Chapters 5 and 6.)

Even if you're climbing with guides, you should be comfortable reading topo maps, compasses, and altimeters. Topographic maps show details of surface configuration—including trails, prominent landmarks, and elevation of wilderness areas and mountains. A compass shows direction and an altimeter records altitude. You can find topo maps, compasses, and altimeters in most outdoor shops and from most guide services. Study books or ask for assistance to learn how to use these invaluable tools.

You'll also want a climbing harness with adjustable leg loops and optional gear slings (see Chapter 6 for information about fitting a harness correctly), a belay device, rescue pulley, an ice hammer, ice screws, several lengths of webbing (slings), extra cord for prusiks, wands (to mark the route or danger areas), a 150- to 165-foot climbing rope, and a four-season or expedition-quality tent (constructed to withstand high winds and heavy snow loads).

You'll also need a helmet made specifically for the sport. Mountaineering *helmets* are commonly made of plastic, fiberglass, or graphite composite materials, and are constructed to protect against blows to the top of the head. Most helmets feature ventilation holes and padded strapping inside for comfortable fit adjustment. Look for helmets with the UIAA (Union Internationale des Associations d'Alpinisme) mark of approval. The Petzl Ecrin Roc is a popular mountaineering helmet.

TOILETRIES

The following is a list of basic personal items you will want to take; you may have your own additional toiletries (e.g., contact lenses and solution).

- **Sunblock and lip protection.** Nothing fries your skin faster than high-altitude sun (there are fewer atmospheric layers between you and the sun) and glare off snow or ice. Use a sunblock with an SPF of 30 or higher and reapply it often. Even brands claiming to be waterproof aren't "rub-proof." Don't use lipstick or lip gloss; use a protective lip salve that is SPF-rated. I once climbed with a woman who did not use any sunblock on her face or lips—within three hours her face looked as though someone had taken a blowtorch to it.

- **Baby wipes.** An indispensable method of maintaining hygiene when there is no running water, shower, or tub!

- **Hairbrush, toothbrush, toothpaste.** Buy the smaller travel sizes to save space and weight.

- **Personal first aid kit.** At a minimum, this should include aspirin or ibuprofen, antacid tablets, bandaids, moleskin, folding scissors, antiseptic cream, and any prescription medications that you take. You might consider tucking in extra tampons or pads for unexpected periods.

- **Toilet paper.** Biodegradable (can be purchased at your local outdoor store).

- **Plastic baggies.** For used kleenex, baby wipes, and other personal trash. Carry all trash off the mountain and dispose of it properly.

OPTIONS

These items will add to the enjoyment of your climb and help bring back special memories.

- **Camera, extra batteries.** Go lightweight and easy-to-use. Unless you are using "disposable" cameras, be sure to take along extra batteries.

- **Paperback book.** For those times when you're tentbound or hutbound by a storm and you tire of hearing "war stories" from the guides or homesick sighs from your climbing partners.

- **Earplugs.** To block out the noise of snoring climbers and for windy nights in the tent.

- **Journal and pencil.** You think you'll remember all the gritty little details, but you won't unless you write it all down. Ink pens can freeze up; it's best to use a pencil. (Some people like to carry a microcassette tape recorder, which means also carrying tapes and extra batteries.)

- **Cell phone.** I really don't want to mention this, but some people insist on bringing a cell phone to check on their husband and kids, buy and sell stock, or whatever. Don't be surprised if the batteries die right away, and don't ask your fellow climbers to say hello to your dog back home.

One way to keep your small stuff organized is to segregate it into small, labeled stuff sacks. Otherwise, those items migrate to the bottom of your pack and take forever to find. Put toiletries in one sack; extra batteries and headlamp in another; book, journal, and pencil in another; bowl, spoon, and mug in another. Put toilet paper in a plastic baggie to keep it dry. After just one outing of rooting around in your pack, you'll quickly find a system that works for you.

You're in shape, you've got your gear. Let's go to the mountain!

Chapter 5

STARTING UP RAINIER

The summer climbing season on Mount Rainier runs from May to the end of September. Francey and Terry elected to climb in early September, the time of year when all the routes on the mountain are well defined. Heavy snows from the previous winter and spring have melted and settled, exposing the network of crevasses that define the glaciated upper terrain. As the snow recedes, the lower mountain reveals a variety of terrain, including rocky glacial moraine, grassy meadows, and wildflowers and heather among scenic rock outcroppings.

A first-time visitor to Mount Rainier in 1885 understandably named the settlement at the base of the mountain Paradise. Today at Paradise, there is a Visitor Information Center, Park Ranger's office, guide headquarters, and a rustic turn-of-the-century hotel, the Paradise Inn. Early in the season, fresh snow commonly covers the parking lot. By September, the snowfall is confined to the upper mountain and the parking lot is dry.

On a bright Monday morning, Francey and Terry reported to the RMI Guide Hut at Paradise, along with eleven other climbers—ten men and one woman—who also had signed up for the five-day mountaineering course. The climbing clients met their five guides; reviewed last-minute gear checks; rented boots, crampons, and ice axes; introduced themselves; and got a quick rundown of what the week's program would encompass. By noon, this process was complete and the group was ready to climb.

Terry and Francey prepare to leave Paradise for Camp Muir.

Heather MacDonald, the lead guide for the seminar, advised everyone to dress comfortably for the five- to six-hour climb to Camp Muir. "The weather is nice, so I'm starting out in a lightweight top, shorts, and a ball cap," she explained. "I'd advise you to do the same. We'll stop for rest breaks about once an hour. You'll have about 10 to 15 minutes to eat something, drink water, and reapply sunscreen. We keep the breaks short so that you don't cool down. In this way, your muscles stay warm. About halfway up to Camp Muir, the wind might come up and turn chilly. Then you might want long pants and a windbreaker. If anyone is having a problem at any time, please tell one of the guides and let us try to help you."

The group carried their backpacks outside to the front of the Guide Hut, where Heather instructed them to stretch their legs and upper body before hoisting their packs. "Don't put on your pack until you see the leader put on his or her pack," she said. "Conserve your energy whenever and however you can. Watch how the guides do it. We know how to conserve energy."

Standing there, with Mount Rainier rising alone in the skyline, dwarfing surrounding peaks, it's helpful to take a few deep breaths to help control the inevitable stomach butterflies. After months of training, investing in new gear, and arranging time off from work, suddenly here's the object of your climbing fantasies looming before you, both magnetic and intimidating. At this moment, you might begin to understand why many seasoned climbers remark that climbing mountains is "90 percent mental exercise." It's easy to get psyched out. Concentrate on paying attention—to both your body and the guides' instructions.

Francey and Terry gathered outside the Guide Hut with the rest of the group. As soon as Heather picked up her backpack, the others slung their loaded packs onto their backs. Francey and Terry grinned at each other and fell into the single-file line that formed behind Heather. The other four guides inserted themselves at various points in the line. As the group advanced uphill, the guides began to silently gauge the potential of each climber.

Senior guide Heather MacDonald demonstrates how to put on a pack.

Terry later commented, "Leaving the Guide Hut, I was wondering if I had trained hard enough, whether I'd be strong enough, whether I could keep up with everyone, whether all these guys were going to be real competitive and maxed out on testosterone, wondering if I had too much in my pack, if my boots would fit well enough to prevent blisters. After all the preparation, here we are, it's now or never. My anxieties were coming on strong, but it was a relief to finally be on our way after months of training." Within a half-hour, Terry fell into a comfortable rhythm of walking and breathing.

The first two hours of the climb, from Paradise at 5,400 feet to Pebble Creek at about 7,800 feet, are regarded by many novices as the most challenging part of the day. During the first hour, the trail switchbacks up the mountain, passing tree line around 6,500 feet and opening to a vista of towering ice walls and rocky escarpments. As climbers advance upward, perspective becomes skewed and the mountain seems to grow more massive as you climb onto its flanks. Francey later remarked, "I stopped looking at landmarks while hiking because they never seemed to get closer. I only looked around during breaks. Otherwise, I focused on the boots of the person hiking in front of me."

During these first two hours, the guides showed their clients how to walk using the *rest step* and how to *pressure-breathe*, two techniques developed by early mountaineers that enable climbers to sustain and maximize energy. The techniques also help maintain a steady pace.

The trail becomes steeper as it enters the Muir Snowfield, a permanent snowfield above Paradise on the way to Camp Muir. The second rest

HOW TO REST-STEP

. . . .

To do the rest step, swing your front leg forward and put it down with no weight on it, then straighten your rear leg so that the bones are in vertical alignment by locking the knee. Rest your weight on that leg. Then step off the back leg and place it in front with no weight on it for a moment, while locking the new back leg. The second or two involved in making this shift from muscle to bone support gives your leg muscles a rest. NOTE: Be sure that your boot is flat on the snow while resting on your back leg.

rear leg with knee locked; weight is on this leg

as you step, shift weight to the new rear leg

unweighted front leg

The rest step.

HOW TO PRESSURE-BREATHE

To pressure-breathe, first exhale forcefully to empty your lungs and make room for more air when you inhale. Make noise when you exhale: purse your lips as you would to whistle; then, with a quick and forceful exhalation, force out as much air as possible. Then take in a full breath. Do this whenever necessary. At high altitude or during extreme exertion, it's not uncommon to pressure-breathe with every breath. At sea level, you'd hyperventilate using this technique. At higher altitudes, the atmospheric pressure is so low that it's nearly impossible to hyperventilate.

Rest break on the Muir Snowfield. (Terry Austin)

stop is at Pebble Creek. Here, as summer grows warmer, a stream gradually emerges from beneath the snow pack, fed by glacial melt. Climbers fill water bottles, eat snacks, reapply sunscreen, and take in the view while the guides continue their evaluation.

Some climbers turn back at Pebble Creek, most commonly from exhaustion or leg cramps. Here is where you begin to notice whether or not your pack is overloaded. The trail from the Muir Snowfield to Camp Muir leads straight up the mountain instead of switchbacking. If a climber has to turn back, a guide accompanies him or her to Paradise. With a 35- to 40-pound pack on their backs, Francey and Terry felt the benefits of their bleacher workouts.

"Physically, I felt well prepared, which helped my confidence," Francey stated. "I didn't have any problem carrying my pack. I just focused on keeping my mental state in synch with my physical capabilities."

Terry added, "The mountain looked so big, I wondered how we could possibly get to the top. Within the first hour, I felt a blister forming on my heel. I began to worry that it would get worse if I didn't stop, but I didn't want to hold up the whole group. I thought of a saying by Kahlil Gibran: 'Pain is the breaking of the shell that encloses our understanding.' That forced me to go inside and focus on the growth and strength I gain from difficult mental and physical challenges. At the first rest break, I took care of the blister. One of the guides showed me how to cover it with duct tape to reduce the friction from my socks and boots. I left my heel swathed in duct tape for five days."

The climb from Paradise to Camp Muir is synonymous with what is called "the approach" to base camp on other mountains. In areas where one cannot drive to the base of a mountain, such as in many foreign countries, the approach can take several days or even a number of weeks, adding to the amount of gear and food necessary to sustain expedition members. Himalayan expeditions commonly use yaks and porters to help carry several tons of supplies to base camp. In South America, mules are often used on the approach.

The proximity of mountains to major cities in the United States makes mountaineering a convenient weekend or week-long pursuit in this country. In the Continental United States, most mountains are within striking distance of cars, and none exceed 14,500 feet in elevation. (California's 14,491-foot Mount Whitney is the highest.) Climbers tackling Alaska's 20,320-foot Mount McKinley are flown from an airstrip in Talkeetna onto the glacier at 7,200 feet. Instead of using the services of yaks and porters, McKinley climbers pull gear and food in specially made sleds and also carry backpacks to provide for an average climb of two to three weeks' duration.

After carrying a full load to base camp, climbers split up their gear and food into lighter loads and ferry them up the mountain to the next higher camp. The routine is to carry a load to the next higher camp and return to base or a lower camp that same day to sleep. The following day, carry the rest of the load to the next higher camp and sleep there. Repeat the process to establish the next higher camp. The routine of "climb high, sleep low" as you advance up a mountain is an important part of the acclimatization process in high altitudes.

During the five-day climbing seminar on Mount Rainier, climbers are based at 10,000-foot Camp Muir. That's where the big-load carrying stops. From there to the summit, packs contain a day's supply of water, a lunch, and extra warm clothes. Most climbers also carry a lightweight camera to capture "hero shots." Sleeping bag, pad, extra clothing, and other items remain at base camp in the wooden bunkhouse. Climbers also have the option

TEN GREAT MOUNTAINS TO CLIMB IN NORTH AMERICA
•••••••••••••••••••

1. Mount Rainier, Washington
2. Mount McKinley, Alaska
3. Mount Whitney, California
4. Mount Shasta, California
5. The Grand Teton, Wyoming
6. Long's Peak, Colorado
7. Mount Orizaba, Mexico
8. Mount Washington, New Hampshire (in winter)
9. Gannett Peak, Wyoming
10. Mount Logan, Canada

of sleeping in a tent or snow cave at Camp Muir, if snow conditions allow. After a hard day's workout on the mountain learning technique, most people elect the simpler option of sleeping in the bunkhouse.

The last stretch up the Muir Snowfield to the bunkhouse at Camp Muir is the most mentally grueling. The route isn't any steeper or longer than other sections of trail, but as Francey remarked earlier, perspective is deceiving. The bunkhouse, visible from the final rest stop, seems to remain at the same distance until you're almost upon it! Instead of familiar objects like trees, telephone poles, and buildings to measure against, you're left with a backdrop of tall ice cliffs and a foreground of seemingly endless snowfields. In time, one adapts to different landmarks and the perspective adjusts. When climbers finally straggle into Camp Muir, they drop their packs and take their sleeping bags into the bunkhouse to capture a spot for them-

Climbers approach the Camp Muir bunkhouse. (Terry Austin)

selves. The cooks have already put jugs of cold water in the bunkhouse for climbers to replenish their water bottles. After the five-hour hike from Paradise, it's already early evening and dinner is soon served.

In addition to a bunkhouse for clients and guides (their respective quarters are separated by a wall), there is a small hut for the Park Ranger, an outhouse, and a cook shack. Supplies are transported to Camp Muir via a helicopter that, in turn, carries off human waste and garbage. The cook shack is well supplied with basic staples and propane. Dinners consist of hearty meals such as spaghetti, stew, turkey and rice, macaroni and cheese. Breakfasts include hot drinks, instant oatmeal, pancakes, or French toast. Lunches are carried to different training sites on the mountain, and usually consist of peanut-butter and jelly sandwiches, pilot-bread biscuits, canned fruit, and cookies, served buffet style. The fare is simple but nourishing, easy to prepare, and, like almost anything eaten outdoors, it tastes great!

Francey and Terry arrived at Camp Muir in high spirits. They took off their packs and hugged each other, then congratulated their climbing partners. A slight cloud cover had moved in, and the guides encouraged the climbers to get their gear sorted for the evening, in the event a storm arrived.

Once settled in the bunkhouse, Terry asked Bonnie Pene, the other woman in the seminar, what made her decide to climb Mount Rainier. "In the fifties, women weren't really encouraged to do this sort of thing, not to mention sports in general," replied 49-year-old Bonnie, who lived in a Seattle suburb. "If we had been, my ambition would have been to be a pro-baseball player. I love stories of pioneer women. I wonder if I would measure up, or survive, if I had to do the same sort of thing. I've always enjoyed being outdoors, hiking and backpacking. But after I got married, I put that stuff on the back burner and got out of shape and didn't think about it. When we moved to the Seattle area about 18 years ago, I saw Mount Rainier and thought it was the most beautiful thing I'd ever seen. I said, 'Someday, I'm going to climb it.'" The climb to Camp Muir had been a challenge for Bonnie, but she quickly settled into the routine of organizing her gear and bunking down for the night.

After dinner, Heather and the guides joined the climbers in the bunkhouse for a knot-tying demonstration and talk. Heather revealed that this climb would be her 107th of Mount Rainier. Some of the more senior guides have summited the mountain more than 300 times during their career. The mountain offers so much challenge and diversity, none of them seem to tire of climbing it.

After the guides demonstrated how to tie several basic knots—regular overhand, figure eight, butterfly, fisherman's, girth and clove hitches, bowline, and prusik—they passed around rope and encouraged the climbers to practice. Then Heather prepped the group for their first night on the mountain.

"It's our first night up here and we're at 10,000 feet," Heather said. "Acclimatization is a very individual thing. Some people might be able to sleep right through the night and feel just like they do at sea level. Others might not sleep so well tonight. Your first night at altitude might be a little restless, you might have a headache—that's normal. One way to take care of that headache is to eliminate the possibility of dehydration. Keep a water bottle by your bunk so that you can stay hydrated through the night. In addition, pressure-breathe or at least breathe deeply. These things will help."

Heather added, "If your appetite tonight and tomorrow morning isn't up to snuff, that's also normal. These are mild symptoms of 'mountain sickness,' but it's no big deal. By the second night, you'll probably feel better. If not, tell us and we'll help you. Also, if you wake up in the morning feeling a little slow and head-achy, just get up and start moving around. As soon as your blood starts pumping, you'll begin to feel better."

Heather explained that at night, when you lie down, your respiratory rate drops to what it is at sea level. This causes the

(continued on page 60)

SERIOUS WOMEN CLIMBERS

Two other women besides Heather have climbed Mount Rainier more than 100 times: Marty Hoey and Cate Casson, both RMI guides. Hoey was one of the first female guides in the United States. She died in a fall on a 1982 Mount Everest expedition. Casson is still guiding with Heather on Mount Rainier, Mount McKinley, and Aconcagua (in Argentina). Together, Heather and Cate guided an all-woman ascent of Mount McKinley in 1995 and a coed group in 1997.

THE SEVEN BASIC KNOTS A CLIMBER SHOULD MASTER

There are basically three types of knots: knots for the end of a rope, knots for the middle, and knots that join two ropes together. These are the seven basic knots a climber should master:

Regular overhand. This is used most often to back up or secure loose rope ends after another knot.

overhand knot backing up a figure eight

Figure eight. This knot is most commonly done as an interwoven figure eight and used to tie in to an anchor or to the harness of the climber on the end of a rope. It also can be used to attach two ends of rope, by making a figure eight in one end and reweaving the other end of rope through it, finishing off with an overhand knot. A figure eight on a *bight* (a section of the rope anywhere but on the ends) creates a loop in the middle of the rope.

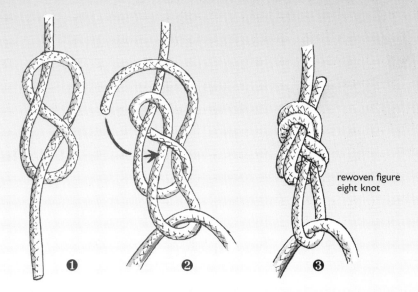

rewoven figure eight knot

Butterfly. This is the preferred knot for the middle person(s) on the rope because it can take a load or fall on either end without coming undone.

butterfly knot

Fisherman's: This knot is also good for joining together two ropes, most commonly done as a "double fisherman's." For rappels, it is less bulky than a rewoven figure eight.

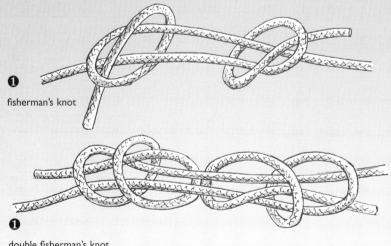

fisherman's knot

double fisherman's knot

(continued on page 58)

THE SEVEN BASIC KNOTS A CLIMBER SHOULD MASTER

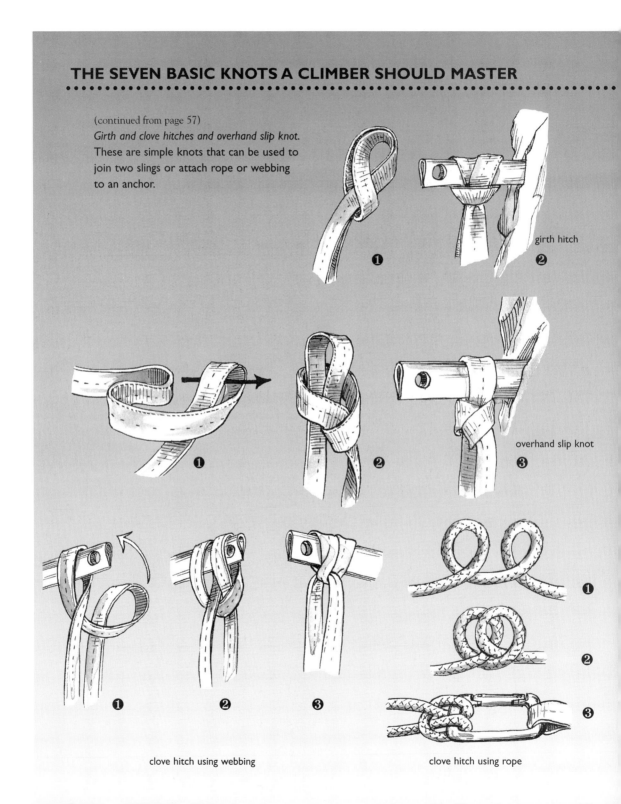

(continued from page 57)
Girth and clove hitches and overhand slip knot.
These are simple knots that can be used to
join two slings or attach rope or webbing
to an anchor.

girth hitch

❶   ❷

❶   ❷   overhand slip knot   ❸

❶   ❷   ❸

❶   ❷   ❸

clove hitch using webbing   clove hitch using rope

Bowline. This knot makes a loop at the end of a rope that will not slip and is good for securing the rope to an anchor or, rewoven, it can be tied into a seat harness.

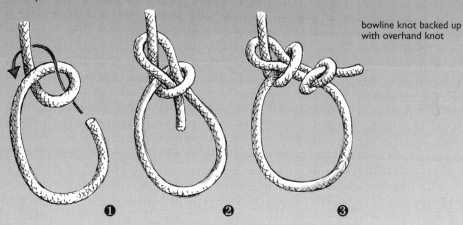

bowline knot backed up
with overhand knot

① ② ③

Prusik. This knot is used to attach an accessory cord of 5- to 7-mm perlon (smaller in diameter than the climbing rope) to a climbing rope. It is used also to create a sling to help raise or lower people and equipment during rescues. This same sling can be used to create a "step" to climb up a rope.

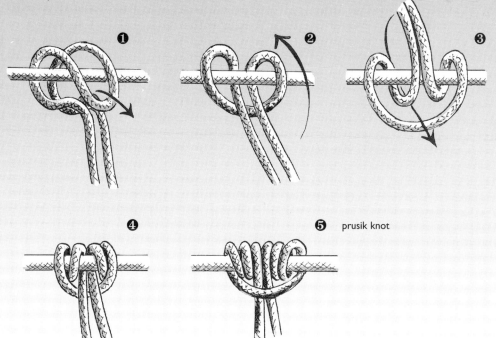

① ② ③

④ ⑤ prusik knot

TYPES OF ROPE
• • • • • • • • • • • • • • • • • • •

During the early days of mountaineering, ropes were made of
natural fibers, such as hemp
and sisal. Nylon ropes were
developed during World War
II. Today, mountaineers use
kernmantle rope, composed of a
core of braided nylon filaments
encased in a smooth nylon
sheath. Some ropes (called
dry ropes) are also chemically
treated to keep them from
absorbing moisture and
becoming heavy. Guide services commonly use thicker
(i.e., 10.5- or 11-mm) ropes
because they hold up longer
under frequent use. Individual
experienced mountain
climbers might opt for a
lighter-weight 9- or 10-mm
rope, depending on route
conditions.

physiological mechanisms in your body to go on red alert, produc-
ing the symptoms of mountain sickness (see page 61 for more on
altitude sickness).

"Drink at least three quarts of water a day while you're up
here on the mountain," she added. "Please don't take any sleeping pills. They defeat the purpose of acclimatizing by lowering
your respiratory rate. A little Tylenol or Advil for aches and
pains is okay."

She outlined the plan for the following day. "We'll get up
around 7 o'clock. Breakfast will happen pretty soon afterwards.
I'll give you clothing recommendations then. The weather up
here changes fast, so we'll wait until tomorrow to see how we
should dress. After breakfast, we'll head out to a nearby slope to
learn and practice self-arrest, cramponing, and rope travel. In
the afternoon, we'll take a glacier walk—give everyone a feel for
that, talk about glaciers and route-finding.

"I'm going to listen to the weather report tonight. My gut
feeling right now is that the weather will probably hold for us to
climb to the summit on Thursday. We'll train Tuesday, do
crevasse rescue and ice climbing on Wednesday. That's the
plan, but we have to be flexible in case the weather changes. My
job is to be an interpreter. We have to listen to the mountain.
The mountain dictates your schedule. Always listen to the
mountain."

Having arrived at Camp Muir feeling strong and motivated, Francey and Terry fell asleep that night, listening.

ALTITUDE-RELATED ILLNESSES

Altitude affects people in different ways. Some people feel mild symptoms of altitude sickness at 5,000 feet. Others don't feel any effects until above 8,000 feet. Physical conditioning doesn't seem to matter much, since fit climbers are as much at risk as out-of-shape beginners. Altitude sickness is at best a nuisance and at worst life-threatening if not treated immediately by descending at least 1,000 feet or lower on the mountain.

There are three forms of altitude sickness: Acute Mountain Sickness (AMS), High Altitude Pulmonary Edema (HAPE), and High Altitude Cerebral Edema (HACE).

The symptoms of Acute Mountain Sickness (AMS) include difficulty in sleeping, mild to severe headache, fatigue, nausea, lack of appetite, dizziness, and shortness of breath. Vomiting may accompany these symptoms.

To minimize these effects, practice pressure-breathing to take in as much oxygen as possible, increase hydration, take aspirin or ibuprofen for headache or, if symptoms are persistently severe, stop your ascent until symptoms disappear. If severe symptoms such as vomiting, extreme headache, or dizziness don't disappear after treatment or rest, descend to a lower altitude right away. If after treatment (including pressure breathing and increased hydration) mild symptoms don't disappear in 24 hours, descend to a lower altitude.

High Altitude Pulmonary Edema (HAPE) is created by a leakage of fluid into the lungs, restricting breathing. This is a serious condition requiring medical care. I've seen a case of HAPE at 13,800 feet—the climber started a trek to base camp with a cold; as she climbed higher, the cold intensified and she developed HAPE and had to be evacuated. Others have reported the condition at lower altitudes. HAPE usually comes on slowly. Early symptoms resemble AMS: headache, nausea, lack of appetite, dizziness, shortness of breath, and general weakness. As the condition intensifies and the lungs begin to fill with fluid, the victim will feel increased lethargy as well as anxiety from inability to breathe properly. The pulse will race, exertion will be difficult, and a persistent cough will develop. The cough may sound dry at first, then graduate to a "wet" cough. The victim may cough up a watery, pink sputum. The lungs may produce a gurgling or crackling sound. These are severe symptoms that require immediate descent and medical care. Without descent, the victim will become comatose, with death following in a matter of hours. Supplemental oxygen may bring some relief but should not be used in place of descending. The victim must be assisted to a lower altitude at once.

High Altitude Cerebral Edema (HACE) is swelling of the brain in reaction to high altitude. Early symptoms include difficulty in walking and maintaining balance, and often withdrawal from others. Victims might remain in their tents, not eating, talking, or taking bathroom breaks. Disorientation, confusion, and hallucinations are common. Severe headache, nausea, and vomiting may precede worse symptoms. To test for early signs of HACE, ask the victim to walk a straight line heel-to-toe. If the patient loses balance, HACE must be suspected. As with HAPE, if descent to lower altitude is not undertaken immediately, the victim will lapse into coma. Supplemental oxygen will help relieve symptoms, but only temporarily.

Certain drugs can help alleviate symptoms before or during descent, but these should be given only by medical professionals. It is wise to take a mountaineering first aid or wilderness

(continued on page 62)

ALTITUDE-RELATED ILLNESSES

(continued from page 61)
medicine course to familiarize yourself with altitude-related sicknesses, treatment, and prevention.

One of the best methods of prevention is to acclimatize slowly as you move from camp to camp (carry a partial load to a higher camp, descend to a lower camp to sleep before moving to the higher camp), pressure-breathe to increase oxygen intake, use the rest step to conserve energy, drink lots of fluids during exertion as well as during rest periods, and eat sufficient amounts of high-carbohydrate foods. Avoid alcohol, narcotic painkillers, and sleeping pills, which tend to dehydrate the body and interfere with natural breathing. Never undertake a climb when suffering from a cold or flu: you will not get *better* as you move to higher altitudes, where oxygen levels decrease in your body. If signs of altitude sickness persist despite prevention and treatment, realize that it isn't your day on the mountain. Descend and come back another time.

Chapter 6

SCHOOL FOR MOUNTAINEERS

After a good night's sleep in their bunks at Camp Muir, Francey and Terry awakened early, ready to begin "climbing school." For the next two days, their climbing class would concentrate on learning how to travel as safely as possible on glaciers, a new experience for even the most seasoned backpacker.

When hiking on dirt and rock trails, the terrain underfoot essentially remains firm. Snow can smooth out a brush- or rock-covered trail, but it also can vary in consistency and surface quality, from a light dusting of powder to a firm-packed surface to rock-hard ice. During the course of a day, conditions can change as solar radiation melts firm snow and causes slush that, in turn, ices up overnight. In addition, a seemingly firm snowpack can create a crusty surface with soft snow beneath, causing the climber to plunge in up to the knee or thigh with every exhausting step (i.e., postholing). Or, the snow pack can suddenly slide out from under the climber in an avalanche or collapse to reveal a crevasse underneath. For these reasons, when climbing on glaciers, climbers often find themselves learning to walk all over again!

During the first day of climbing school, Francey and Terry and their group would learn *self-arrest*, a crucial technique designed to stop a fall—of yourself or a climbing partner. They also would learn how to use harnesses, crampons, and ice axes, and how to hike on a glacier while roped to other climbers.

GLACIER TRAVEL TIPS

Be vigilant in maintaining your balance to prevent falling or sliding. Climb with your eyes. The rest step, proper foot placement, and coordinated ice-axe use are techniques that contribute to safe travel on snow or glaciated terrain.

Know the terrain. Learn to read topography maps through reading books or taking courses on the subject. Be sure you understand where your trail leads—to the edge of a cliff, a ridge, a rock abutment?

Learn how to spot hidden crevasses. Telltale signs include a crease or depression in the snow. After a snowfall, new snow can fill in a sagging trench and cause it to blend in with the surrounding terrain. While walking, look out to each side for open cracks that could hint at a crevasse extending beneath your route. If you see that the crevasse narrows to a close at one end, head for that end and walk around the crevasse. Keep the rope between climbers taut at all times. It is better to add a little distance to your climb than to risk the danger of a crevasse fall.

Study snow bridges carefully. Formed by deep winter snow hardened by wind, snow bridges stretch between the walls of a crevasse. Don't assume that the one you crossed in the morning will still be stable after a day of thawing in the sun. If there is no other way around or across a crevasse, the rope leader should venture out on the snow bridge—slowly, carefully, cautiously—using her ice axe to probe for the firmest route across. At the same time, the other climbers on the rope should keep the rope taut as the leader crosses.

Another technique for crossing snow bridges is to use solid snow anchors to belay each climber across the snow bridge. The proper snow anchor is determined by the conditions of the snow pack, the angle of the slope, and the direction of the load, or *pull*.

Heather leads the rope team on a glacier walk. (Terry Austin)

The climber immediately behind the leader sets a strong anchor—either a sitting belay with bollard, two equalized snow pickets, or a deadman—and then attaches herself to the anchor (see page 69 in this chapter). Both the climbers and the anchor should be set back from the lip of the crevasse for safety. Each succeeding climber in the group uses the anchor in the same manner. The last person across the snow bridge may be belayed by the climbers who have already crossed.

Don't venture into known avalanche areas. In addition to learning from mountain guides and experienced climbing partners, study books or take a course on evaluating avalanche-prone areas (see Chapter 10, Resources, for suggestions). Many parameters go into evaluating avalanche danger, including the steepness or angle of the slope, the direction it faces (its *aspect*), whether the slope is smooth or interrupted with trees and rocks, the amount of new snowfall, and the effect of temperature changes. Equally important is to consider the human factor, from your level of expertise to the level of risk you are willing to undertake. During training, observe and ask questions if you don't understand the reasoning behind route selection.

After a hearty breakfast, Heather advised everyone to dress in layers of lightweight thermal underwear, with a fleece jacket, outerwear pants, and jacket. The day had dawned fair but chilly. In addition to a warm hat and gloves, each climber would pack an insulated parka to wear between training sessions. Lightweight gloves would be worn at all times, even in warm weather, to protect hands from abrasion from snow and ice and to increase a climber's chance of holding onto her ice axe during a fall. Heather mentioned that on a regular mountaineering outing, a climber would never leave camp without additional protection from changing weather. Developing a versatile, protective clothing ensemble is just as important as learning climbing technique.

One of the climbers remained behind while the others followed the guides out onto the mountain. After a restless night, Bonnie had awakened feeling ill. She had a racing heartbeat accompanied by bouts of dizziness. Thinking that it might be the effects of the altitude gain from Paradise to Camp Muir, Heather advised Bonnie to remain at the bunkhouse to rest and drink plenty of fluids while the rest of the climbing party spent the day in training. At the end of the day, Heather would reevaluate Bonnie's condition.

The guides led the climbers to a hill behind the cook shack to practice self-arrest. During initial training, the climbers would not wear crampons or harnesses. As Heather explained, "When you have crampons on and are carrying an ice axe, you become a lethal weapon. We want you to become comfortable with the ice axe first, then we'll add the other gear."

The climbers split into three teams, each with one or two guides, and climbed to the top of a gentle slope. The guides then proceeded to demonstrate how to use an ice axe and your body to stop yourself from sliding downhill after a fall. They slid every which way—feet first on their backs, then stomachs, then repeated the process going head first on backs and stomachs. Each climber practiced several times until the guides were satisfied that everyone understood the technique. (See sidebar on page 75.)

"Strength is important in self-arrest," Heather explained, "but even more important is proper technique. If you do it right, you can stop yourself and other members of your rope team from sliding down the mountain."

While heading back to Camp Muir for lunch, the climbers were taught how to walk downhill, using the *plunge step*.

Plunge-stepping downhill.

BELAYING

Belaying is a technique in which one climber safeguards another climber from a long fall. The two climbers are connected by a rope. If one climber falls, the second climber uses friction around the body or through a belaying device to slow down and stop the rope and thus the fall.

The belayer, who must be attached to one or more anchors, passes the rope around her hips and through the carabiner on her seat harness (see page 69 in this chapter for instruction on setting anchors; harnesses are discussed on page 70 and in Chapter 7). One hand guides the rope as it plays out to the climber. The other hand, the one closest to the body and on the free end of the rope, acts as the brake hand. With the rope running around your hips and through the carabiner on your harness, and with one hand creating a brake, an incredible amount of friction is created. This technique can be used standing or sitting.

Make certain that your brake hand never leaves the rope. To pull in slack, the brake hand and guide hand work in concert. While the guide

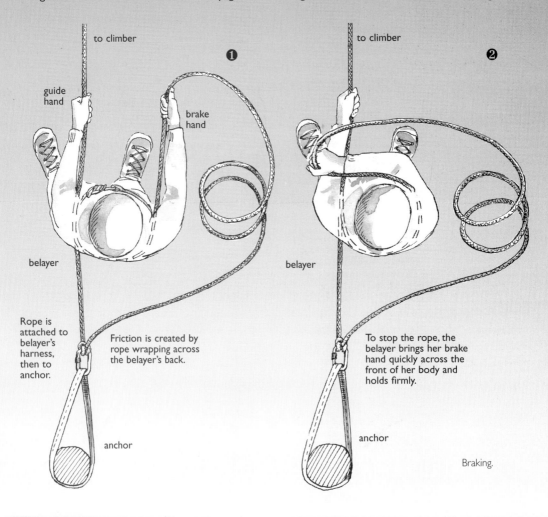

to climber

❶

guide hand

brake hand

belayer

Rope is attached to belayer's harness, then to anchor.

Friction is created by rope wrapping across the belayer's back.

anchor

to climber

❷

belayer

To stop the rope, the belayer brings her brake hand quickly across the front of her body and holds firmly.

anchor

Braking.

hand pulls the rope toward the body, the brake hand pulls rope away from the body. Then the guide hand extends back out to grab both pieces of rope, and the brake hand slides over the rope back toward the body to repeat the process until the slack is diminished.

To arrest a fall and prevent the rope from running out, quickly bring your braking arm across the front of your body and hold the rope firmly. By bringing the rope across the front of your body, you increase the wrap and also the

friction. Any other position can cause the rope to unwrap and create an unstable situation.

There are many mechanical belay devices on the market that help increase friction on the rope. I suggest that you first become familiar with using your body and hands to control the friction of a basic belay and experience holding the weight of another climber before relying on a mechanical device. With either system, the brake hand is the crucial component in stopping the rope.

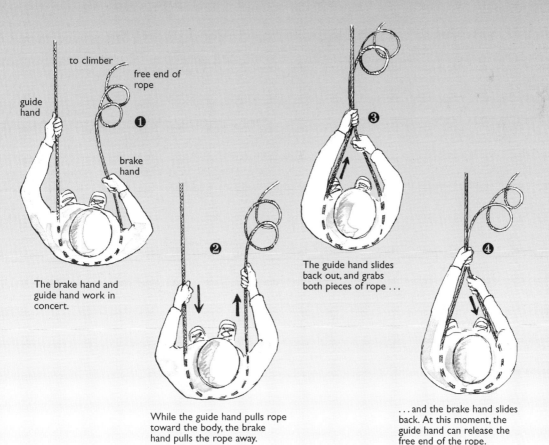

to climber

free end of rope

guide hand

❶

brake hand

The brake hand and guide hand work in concert.

❷

While the guide hand pulls rope toward the body, the brake hand pulls the rope away.

❸

The guide hand slides back out, and grabs both pieces of rope . . .

❹

. . . and the brake hand slides back. At this moment, the guide hand can release the free end of the rope.

Pulling in the rope. (Harness is not shown for sake of simplicity of illustration.)

THE RUNNING BELAY

• • • • • • • • • • • • • • • • • • • •

Another technique for protecting climbers on moderately difficult sections is the use of a *running belay*. This is a time-saving technique that allows a rope team to move simultaneously while still being anchored to the mountain. The lead climber in the group ascends, placing anchors (i.e., snow pickets or ice screws) and using a carabiner to clip the climbing rope into each anchor. Each climber on the rope unclips before the anchor and reattaches on the other side. The rear climber removes each anchor. This process can be repeated as many times as necessary to ascend a difficult section.

This involves a wide stance, knees about shoulder width apart, body weight centered over the feet to prevent falling over backwards. Stretch out your hands straight in front of your body, elbows slightly bent, and hold the ice axe in one or both hands as needed to maintain balance.

Terry observed, "It felt very weird to be dropped head first down a slope to see if you could stop yourself, but I discovered that a lot of it was instinctual, to flip over onto my stomach. Plunge-stepping also felt comfortable and made a lot of sense. Each technique we learned added a little more to my level of confidence."

She added, "Our group was great, really helpful and supportive, easy to talk to. I wasn't drowning in a sea of testosterone after all."

In the afternoon, following lunch at Camp Muir, Heather and the other guides demonstrated the use of crampons and harnesses. Heather explained the proper use of the harness: "You want to wear it over your base layer of clothing, or over the least amount of clothing you can. Never wear it over your parka. If you get too much clothing between your body and the harness, when you have to remove a layer or two, you create a baggy harness that can slip off in a fall."

Heather continued: "The waistbelt of the harness goes above the hip bones and below the ribs, not on your hips. Again, if you fall, the harness could come off. Cinch it down until it's snug. You should be able to slip your hand under the waistbelt, but not your fist. Double the belt back through the buckle to keep it from slipping out of the buckle.

"The leg loops don't need to be as snug as the waistbelt. Just make them comfortable, and also thread the belt back through each buckle to keep it secure. The keeper sling in the back of the harness goes from the left leg up through the waistbelt and over to the right leg. This sling holds up the back of the leg loops so they don't droop around your knees."

Heather added that there are lots of specialized harnesses now on the market, made specifically for rock climbing or alpine climbing. "This sport is very gear-intensive," she said. "Learn how to use the basic gear and clothing before you start adding other stuff."

SNOW ANCHORS

• •

In addition to belaying, the ability to set and use *snow anchors* is also vital to climbing on glaciers and learning crevasse rescue. Anchors can be created with slings attached to the climbing rope from snow pickets, aluminum flukes, or ice screws embedded in the snow, or from skis or ice axes buried in soft snow. An ice axe thrust vertically into the ground is not a reliable anchor to carry the load and protect the life of a fallen climber. Three of the most commonly used anchors are *bollards*, *deadmen*, and *pickets*.

To make a bollard, dig a trench in the snow in an oval pattern, with the narrow portion of the oval pointing toward the direction of pull. In hard snow, you might have to use an ice axe to dig the trench; in soft snow, you can use your boot or gloved hands. In really soft snow, the mound you create might have to be almost 2 feet high to be effective.

Bollards take longer to establish than hammering in a snow picket or burying an ice axe or snow picket (to make a deadman), but they

Lou Whittaker demonstrates belay technique from a sitting bollard.

create a reliable anchor in all types of snow for belaying or rappelling. A belayer can sit behind the bollard and execute a hip belay, or a sling can be placed around the bollard and attached to the climbing rope with a carabiner to work as an anchor for rappelling or as a backup for a rescue operation. (See Chapter 7 for more information on anchors.)

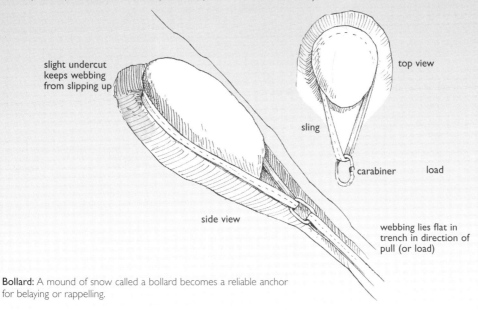

slight undercut keeps webbing from slipping up

top view

sling

side view

carabiner   load

webbing lies flat in trench in direction of pull (or load)

Bollard: A mound of snow called a bollard becomes a reliable anchor for belaying or rappelling.

HARNESSES

. . . .

Some companies, including Arc'Teryx, Misty Mountain Works, Blue Water, and Black Diamond, now make harnesses contoured to a woman's anatomy and in women's sizes. Regardless of what size you think you are, be sure to try on a harness before making the purchase. After buckling the waistbelt, there should be enough belt left to double back through the buckle with a couple of inches remaining to prevent the belt from slipping out. The leg loops should be adjustable or allow enough room for you to raise your knees or squat comfortably without getting pinched by the loops.

Most harnesses provide gear loops for attaching extra carabiners, prusiks, ascenders, belay devices, and rescue pulleys. Follow the manufacturer's directions for wearing and tying into a harness.

Next were crampons. Heather explained the two types—hinged and rigid. "Hinged crampons like the ones we use here are great for all-around use. We use these on Rainier, McKinley, Aconcagua, and in the Himalayas. There also are rigid-frame crampons that are more ideal for technical ice climbing, as they give more support for the foot and ankle. But in soft snow, the snow will ball up in the frame. Even in the hinged crampons, you'll get some snow accumulation, but you just knock it out with your ice axe."

Heather added, "Here on Rainier, we use strap-on crampons instead of step-ins. Step-in crampons are faster to put on and take off, but you have to make sure you get an exact fit or they'll slip off your boot. On a mountain like McKinley, the step-ins don't work with overboots. That's why we use strap-on crampons there. Once a strapping system is in place, it's on there for good."

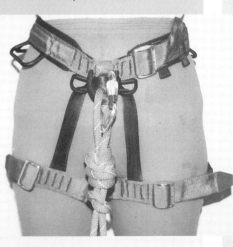

Harness showing rope attached with **figure-eight knot,** backed up with overhand knot.

Harness showing rope attached with **butterfly knot.**

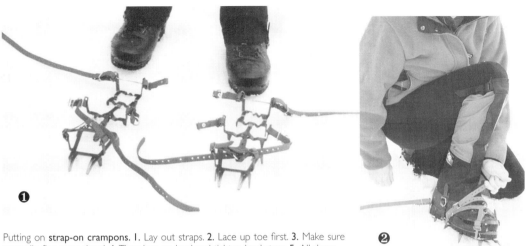

Putting on **strap-on crampons**. 1. Lay out straps. 2. Lace up toe first. 3. Make sure straps lie flat, not twisted. 4. Then lace up heel and tighten heel strap. 5. All done—straps are flat with ends tucked away.

Heather instructed the climbers to kneel on one knee at a time as they fastened their crampons to their boots. "Put your toe in first, then pop in the heel. Take the long strap and go to the inside middle ring first, pull it nice and tight. Then thread the strap through the toe ring and pull it tight. Next, go to the outside middle ring and pull it tight so that you can't get a finger between the strap and your boot. Make sure the straps are flat, not twisted. Then take the strap through the back ring, wrapping the extra strap around the front of the ankle and through the buckle. Crank down hard on that buckle. Tuck any leftover strap under the fixed straps to get them out of the way. You want to end up with a clean profile so that nothing gets stuck on the tooth of your crampon."

Each climber followed Heather's example, step by step. Then it was time to learn to walk. Heather showed

NEW WAYS OF WALKING

• • • • • • • • • • • • • • • • • •

When wearing crampons, it's important to keep the feet flat on the snow to gain maximum purchase. On steep uphill slopes, use the duck walk to sustain strength by alternating muscle groups.

The duck walk involves pointing the feet uphill and splaying them slightly outward. Take short steps and use your ice axe as a second point of balance. Roll your ankles downhill to accommodate the angle of the slope.

The crossover step advances you up the mountain sideways. Cross one foot over the other in short steps. Stomp your foot flat into the snow as you step and point the toe of your boot slightly downhill for a more comfortable position. Again, roll the ankle downward to accommodate the angle of the slope.

Use the rest step with either technique to increase efficiency and maximize strength.

Rigid crampons are made of a fixed frame and built for technical ice climbing. Hinged crampons flex at the instep and are built to accommodate the natural motion of walking. (See illustration on page 45 for three types of crampons.)

(continued on page 73)

the group how to walk so that the crampon is always kept flat against the snow. On steep terrain, use the *crossover step*, and walk up the mountain sideways. Or, use the *duck walk*, also called the *herringbone*, which involves splaying the feet out . . . like a duck! "Alternate the duck walk and crossover step when you're climbing steep slopes," said Heather. "In this way, you'll use different muscle groups and not wear yourself out."

For the glacier walk, the climbers also donned helmets. "They should be snug on your head so they don't flop forward or backward," said Heather. "Use the chin strap and wear the helmet at all times while you're on a glacier."

The climbers roped up together in teams of four and five, with a guide at the front and rear of each rope. Heather stated, "Watch where you step in crampons and don't step on the rope. If you puncture the core, you'll weaken the rope. If this happens, tie a butterfly knot, figure eight, or overhand knot to get the damaged piece out of the main tension area."

Heather explained how the rope acts as a safety device. "Let's say I'm walking up a slope and I take a fall that I can't arrest. My team hits the anchor position and I'm stopped. If I fall into a crevasse, the rest of the team hits the deck in the self-arrest position and stops me from falling or pulling in the person behind me."

In addition, Heather explained, the rope is a communication

Heather demonstrates proper foot placement for **cross-stepping**.
(Terry Austin)

Proper stance for **duck walk** or **herringbone**.

line. "Hold your ice axe in your uphill hand and the piece of rope coming out of your harness loosely in your downhill hand. Keep your arm relaxed at your side. You'll be able to feel when the climber behind you slows down. You won't have to be turning around constantly and yelling, 'What's going on?' Try to keep vocal communication to a minimum when climbing. Concentrate on breathing and stepping. Keep a minimal amount of slack between you and the person in front of you. If a climber falls with too much slack in the rope, extra force is created by falling body weight and will possibly yank in the climber behind him or her. Minimize that risk by using a proper rope interval [i.e., 30 to 40 feet]. Then, if you or the climber in front of you falls in a crevasse, you might only go in up to your hips."

After the glacier walk, Francey commented, "We stepped across some really deep crevasses and I got pretty nervous. Heather took us up a ridge on a rocky scree trail that was only wide enough for our feet. She stopped and told us to take off our packs, but there was no place to put them because the trail dropped off on both sides. I sat on mine. Heather pointed out Disappointment Cleaver and I whipped my head around because that had been the big nemesis in my mind and I was really

(continued on page 78)

NEW WAYS OF WALKING

(continued from page 72)

There are different kinds of strap configurations: some have a separate set of straps that attach to the front of the boot and another set that attaches the rear of the crampon by wrapping around the boot ankle. To achieve a snug fit, straps should be kept flat and never allowed to twist (see photos on page 71).

Whether you decide to use strap-on or step-in crampons, try them on with the boots you plan to wear before you make a purchase. Not all boots are compatible with all crampons. If you plan to do climbing that involves the use of insulating overboots, also wear those while fitting crampons. The use of overboots will narrow your crampon selection to strap-on models only.

Cross-stepping with ice axe on steep slopes: 1. Turn sideways to the slope and ascend diagonally. 2. Keep feet flat—you may want to point them slightly downhill to do so. 3. Keep your weight over your crampons instead of leaning into the slope.

PROPER ICE-AXE TECHNIQUES

When climbing, hold the ice axe so that you'll be ready to arrest a slide if you fall. Hold the axe with the adze pointing forward, thumb underneath the adze, the palm of the hand wrapped over the top of the pick, and one or two fingers running down the shaft. On flat terrain, you can carry the axe by the shaft parallel to the ground, but make certain the spike points forward and the pick points down.

Always keep one hand on your ice axe. Carry it in the uphill hand; you'll arrest to the downhill side. Practice becoming equally skilled in handling the ice axe with both your right and left hands. If you have to stop on a steep slope to make a gear adjustment, plant your ice axe firmly in the ground and clove hitch your climbing rope around it to create an anchor while you make adjustments. Be aware of your ice axe at all times.

When switchbacking up a slope on a rope team and approaching a corner, drop the rope about 5 to 10 feet from the corner, and step over it so that the rope is on the ground on the uphill side. To switch your ice axe from one hand to another at a corner, plunge the ice axe into the ground at the corner, place your new uphill hand on the head, and simultaneously release the axe with your new downhill hand. Lift the axe in your new uphill hand, pick up the rope in your new downhill hand, and proceed. If done properly, the rope team's pace is maintained and no excess slack builds up between you and your rope partners.

Proper ice axe grip. **Left:** Adze points forward, pick to the rear, ready to self-arrest. **Right:** Carrying on flat terrrain. You will notice that some climbers carry the axe with pick forward, which can delay the self-arrest procedure.

SELF-ARREST TECHNIQUE
• •

Don't take this training lightly. Good self-arrest skills can save your life and the lives of your fellow climbers. At the first indication of a fall, the falling climber (or anyone witnessing the fall) yells, "Falling!" to alert the other climbers on the rope.

Climbers on the rope of the falling climber should immediately assume the self-arrest position by dropping to one knee, driving the pick of the ice axe into the snow, kicking buckets into the snow with the feet, and pulling the shaft of the ice axe up to the hip. This is the strongest anchor point a climber can create without the use of ice screws or stakes. This action can prevent the entire rope team from sliding down the mountain and falling into a crevasse.

While yelling "Falling!," the falling climber also immediately goes into self-arrest position. No matter which way you fall—backwards, forwards, on your back, or on your face—the goal is to maneuver yourself into the self-arrest position, lying head uphill and face down, feet pointing toward the direction of pull, with the ice axe beneath you.

If you have been carrying the ice axe correctly, you already have one hand on the head of the ice axe. With your other hand, grab the shaft of the axe near the spike to prevent it from swinging wildly and creating injury.

To achieve arrest, roll toward the head of the axe. If you roll toward the spike, it could catch in the snow before you have a chance to anchor the pick and flip out of your hands. Plant the pick firmly in the ground and maneuver your body so that the adze is just above your shoulder. Press your chest and shoulder down on the shaft, and pull up the end of the shaft firmly against the opposite hip. Keep your head face down (to help keep your body weight over the head of the axe), back slightly arched, legs stiff and spread apart, and toes digging into the snow (similar to a push-up position).

(continued on page 76)

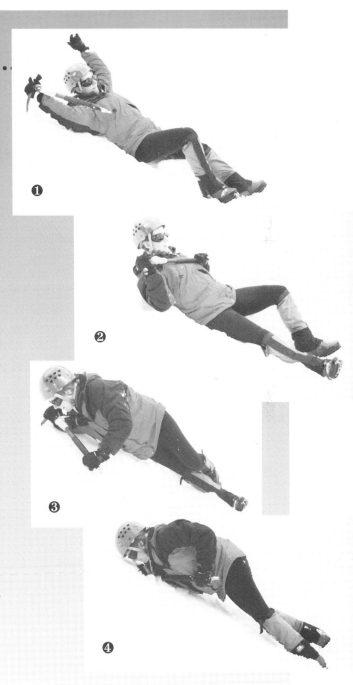

Self-arrest, feet first on back: 1. Yell "falling!" 2. Gain control of the ice axe. 3. Roll toward the head of the axe, and plant the pick firmly. 4. Dig in your feet and pull the shaft up against your hip, keeping your weight over the head of the axe.

SELF-ARREST TECHNIQUE

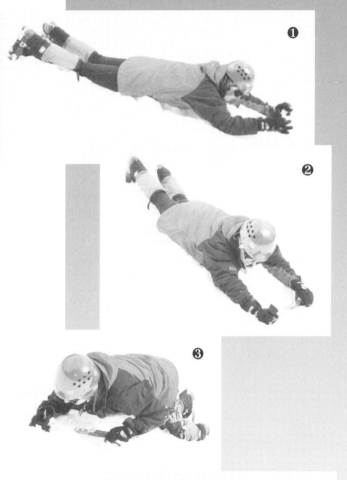

❶

❷

❸

❹

Self-arrest, head first on stomach: **1.** Gain control of the ice axe downhill in front of you. **2.** Maneuver feet downhill. **3.** Plant ice axe and dig in feet. **4.** Achieve self-arrest position.

(continued from page 75)
Here are some suggestions for achieving self-arrest position from different angles:

- **Falling feet first on your face.** You're already halfway into position; now, bury the pick and get your body over the shaft, head down. Secure the shaft against your hip while digging in your toes.

- **Falling feet first on your back.** Pull the ice axe close to your body, with the shaft crossing your chest diagonally and the head of the axe by your shoulder. Roll toward the pick and aggressively plant it in the snow as you roll onto your stomach to achieve the self-arrest position.

- **Falling head first on your face.** Concentrate on getting your feet downhill by using your axe as a pivot. In this scenario, hold the axe out in front of you. Reach downhill and out to the axe-head side. Bury the pick into the snow and let your body swing around—use your feet and legs to speed up the process, if necessary. As soon as your feet are heading downhill, achieve the self-arrest position.

- **Falling head first on your back.** Again, the pick will serve as a pivot point. But in this instance, you will sit up and reach out to the axe-head side, and bury the pick in the snow near your hip. Roll your chest toward the axe head while working your legs downhill. Then achieve the self-arrest position.

- If you find yourself in loose, deep snow where the ice axe cannot be buried in compact snow, use your hands, elbows, knees, and feet to stop your progress. If you lose your ice axe, clasp your hands together to accumulate snow and create more friction. If your first attempt at self-arrest doesn't slow or stop you, keep trying. Be very aggressive. It's important to act immediately, to slow your fall quickly before gaining speed. You can expect to almost always slide some distance before stopping, even with other members on

Self-arrest, head first on stomach: **1.** Falling climber plants head of ice axe to arrest fall. **2.** The climber's body pivots around the planted ice axe. The fall is slowed or stopped, allowing the climber to dig in the feet and achieve self-arrest. (Keith Gunnar)

flatter terrain near the end of the slope, which may help arrest your fall.

- Understand the limits of self-arrest, which are determined by several factors, including the steepness and length of the slope, your reaction time, your level of experience, and the experience level of your climbing partners. On steep or hard icy slopes, the use of a running belay or fixed anchors increases the safety of a rope team (see page 68 in this chapter).

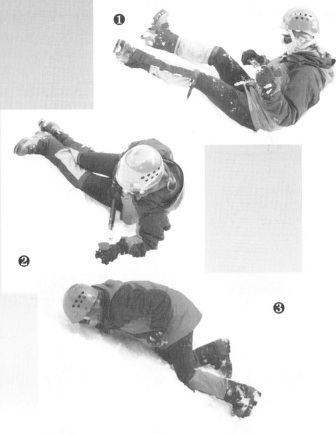

your rope team also in the self-arrest position. The slack and stretch in the rope has to play itself out.

- Remain in the self-arrested anchor position until the condition of all the members of your rope team has been assessed and reported to the rope leader. The next move depends on the result of the fall. If no one is injured or hanging in a crevasse, climbers may get to their feet one by one and resume climbing. If there is an injury or a rescue situation exists, other procedures should be initiated immediately (see Chapter 7).

- If you are climbing unroped, follow the same self-arrest procedures. Without the added security of a rope, you may fall farther and, if you're lucky, hit soft snow or

Self-arrest, head first on back: **1.** Gain control of ice axe, sit up, reach out to side of hip. **2.** Plant ice axe near hip and use a pivot to get your feet downhill. **3.** Achieve self-arrest position.

TESTING THE TECHNIQUE

That last climb on Rainier in 1996, when our party had turned back from the summit, is imprinted in my memory. We descended slowly in low visibility through the cloud that had enveloped the upper mountain. My rope team had just entered a particularly steep traverse (while walking across the face of the hill, I could reach out and touch the side of the mountain). Suddenly, Tim, the climber in front of me, fell. He shouted "Falling!"—as the guides had taught us to do— as he slid toward a crevasse. Immediately, I went into self-arrest, plunging my ice axe into the snow and digging in my crampons to keep myself from also being pulled off the trail. The man on the rope in front of Tim also self-arrested, and together we stopped Tim's fall. With my forehead against the snow, my butt in the air to maintain leverage, I remember thinking, "Hey, this really works." I'd had training in self-arrest but had never, until then, had to use the technique. We remained in our self-arrest positions as Tim quietly climbed back up to the trail and then announced shakily, "Thanks, I'm okay."

"**W**hen you're put in a position where you could die if others don't care, aren't vigilant, aren't experienced, you realize how interdependent we are on each other. In life, we all need a rope team."

—Amber M. Brookman

concerned about climbing it. I could see that the trail up the Cleaver went straight up the face of a rocky ridge. It looked like someone had taken a pencil and drawn a zigzag up the face of the ridge. The trail would blur into the snow and reemerge on the rock. I was really worried about it. Back at camp, I talked to one of the other climbers who had been on the mountain before. He said, 'Don't worry, just don't look over the edge and you'll be okay.' So, now that I had seen the dragon, I was worried about it even more. My goal on this climb was to get above Disappointment Cleaver; after that, the summit would be a bonus."

During this five-day seminar, Francey, Terry, and their climbing group would have the opportunity to collect several bonuses.

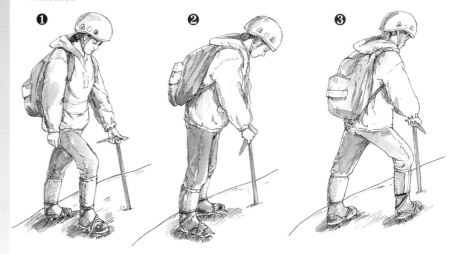

Ice-axe techniques: changing hands at a corner. **1.** Plunge ice axe into snow; keep hand on it. **2.** Place both hands on head of axe as your face uphill. **3.** After you make the turn, remove downhill hand; ice axe is now in uphill hand.

ROPE TRAVEL TIPS

Climbers connected by a single rope comprise a rope team; emphasis is on the word *team*. Travel at a pace that is comfortable for all rope team members. The pace might feel a little slow for some, a little fast for others. If you do not maintain a constant pace, you'll be constantly battling with too much slack or a taut rope, climbers getting pulled off balance, or having to wait while slack is taken up.

- Hold the end of the rope trailing to the rear lightly in your downhill hand; hold your ice axe in the uphill hand. (The climber at the end of the rope does not need to hold onto the rope.)

- It is dangerous to allow slack in the rope, except at corners where it is unavoidable. The rope should leave one climber's harness and lie on the snow directly in front of her, extending to the next climber. If a fall occurs with slack in the rope, the falling climber will fall farther and faster down a slope, or deeper into a crevasse, increasing the chance of injury. For the other climbers on the rope, this can also mean a greater force of pull on the rope.

- Travel on glaciers with a proper rope interval—at least 30 to 40 feet—between climbers. A minimum of three or more people on a rope is recommended so that there is more than one climber to arrest a ropemate's fall into a crevasse or—in the worst-case scenario—so that there are enough people to conduct a crevasse rescue. Only extremely experienced climbers or professional guides should rope up in pairs on glaciated terrain.

RESCUE TECHNIQUES AND SKILLS

Following the first day of training, Heather spent time after dinner in the bunkhouse going over the agenda for the second day of training. First, she explained why she had decided to send Bonnie, the 49-year-old woman climbing with Terry and Francey, back down to Paradise.

"Her condition hadn't changed by the end of the day," said Heather. "Her heart was still racing, she was still feeling dizzy. We don't want to risk creating an emergency, so we sent her down with a guide. The mountain will be here when she's ready to come back."

Heather then refocused the group on the upcoming day of training. "We'll have a full day tomorrow," she said. "We'll look for some good walls where we can teach you how to set up snow anchors, do crevasse rescue, and some ice climbing."

Rope travel in and near crevasses. (Keith Gunnar)

One of the climbers asked about the wisdom of training in a crevasse. "We'll avoid the bottomless kind," said Heather with a grin.

Francey and Terry fell asleep in their bunks with visions of "crevasse rescue" bouncing around in their heads, realizing that first somebody had to go down into a crevasse in order to be rescued from it. The next morning, a cloud cover had moved in over the mountain, depositing light snow and sleet—adding to the climbers' anxiety. Terry said, "I kept thinking, what have I gotten myself into?"

As fearsome as it may sound, crevasse rescue is the second most-crucial mountaineering technique after self-arrest. Learning how to haul yourself or a climbing partner out of a hole in a glacier is a technique all mountaineers should master and then hope never to have to use.

To demonstrate and practice rescue techniques, Heather and the guides led the climbers to a site where the glacier was scarred by yawning cracks. Terry later remarked, "We were walking around all these crevasses and I thought, 'Wow, we're actually going into one of these.' I was a little anxious, but I also believed that the guides weren't going to put us, knowingly, into a dangerous situation. At one point I asked Heather, 'Is that the crevasse we're going into, does it have my name on it?' She looked at me, frowning, and said, 'All these crevasses could have your name on them.' I got the feeling that she was telling me this wasn't something to joke about."

After finding a suitable crevasse for training—one with a wide opening and a somewhat smooth wall—the guides showed the climbers how to anchor the ropes that would be used in the

Crevasse-rescue training. Who wants to go first? Heather leads rope team to the lip. (Terry Austin)

POSTSCRIPT FROM BONNIE

• • • • • • • • • • • • • • • • • •

After the seminar, Bonnie wrote to Terry: "My doctor and I have come to the conclusion that what happened to me was an overdose of *caffeine*, believe it or not! I know that caffeine can make my heart act up, so I have one cup of coffee in the morning and that's it. I didn't realize the [energy bars and energy gels] that I had experimented with all last month and had guzzled for three days before the climb to get the carbohydrates are all loaded with caffeine! This would not be good even at sea level, but the altitude really accentuated the problem. I was trying to do everything right and give myself the best possible chance of succeeding, and ended up doing the worst possible thing. Oh well … you live and learn new things each time."

Bonnie hadn't given up. She scheduled another climb for the following summer and started working out all over again, adding Tae Kwon Do to her

(continued on page 82)

POSTSCRIPT FROM BONNIE

(continued from page 81)

repertoire to enhance her balance. "The first time I trained for Rainier, I didn't enjoy the running and stair climbing. It was boring," she said. "Now that I have had a little taste of my goal, I look forward to my workouts. A few people have said, 'Haven't you failed enough?' The way I look at it, you don't fail more, you learn more. Each time you go back out there, you learn something new. I am going to climb that mountain." Go girl!

"**M**any glaciers appear so smooth on the surface, it looks like you can just run out there forever, but they're covered with cracks and holes. I think 80 percent of the accidents that occur are the result of people letting down their guard . . . and it happens so quickly."

—Jennifer Herzig, mountaineer and high school teacher

rescue demonstration. Although Francey and Terry watched with increasing anxiety, Francey volunteered to be one of the first climbers lowered into the crevasse. Terry was impressed. "The guides showed us how to set up the whole rescue system, using anchors and pulleys to pull somebody out—you are shown only once. Here we are freaking out about who would be lowered into the crevasse first, and Francey steps up and says, 'I'll do it.' I thought, 'Whoa, that's really brave!' I planned to just sit back and watch a few people, take some pictures, before I volunteered."

The first exercise involved lowering Francey into the crevasse while the remaining climbers on her rope team anchored her "fall." For the purpose of teaching crevasse rescue, the guides attached an extra rope to Francey as a safety backup. In a real-life situation, as soon as other rope-team members see the climber in front of them fall into a crevasse, they immediately go into the self-arrest position, turning away from the direction of pull to arrest the fall.

The guides showed the rope team how to set an anchor and release from self-arrest without endangering Francey's safety. Before releasing from the self-arrest position, the climber on the farthest end of the rope stands up slowly, to make certain that the other climbers can hold the load. The end climber then sets an anchor and attaches the rope to that anchor. The climbers still in self-arrest then get to their feet slowly, to make certain the anchor will hold.

Heather explained that if there is another rope team in the vicinity, it is best for all climbers on the fallen rope to remain in self-arrest while the other rope team sets up the anchor. While the rescue climbers are working up above, they should be tied or clipped to an anchor or belay at all times for safety.

After the anchor is in place, belay one of the climbers to the edge of the crevasse to assess the situation. The climber should approach from off to one side of the rope, to avoid kicking snow or ice down onto the fallen climber. Call to the fallen climber—is she injured, unable to respond? If so, it may be necessary for one climber to be belayed into the crevasse to offer assistance. If the fallen climber can respond, the rescuer on top should first ask if the climber can ice-climb out using her crampons and ice axe on the crevasse wall or climb up the rope using prusiks or mechanical ascenders. If the crevasse lip is undercut, it would be best for the fallen climber to attach two prusik slings or *mechanical ascenders* to the rope, and prepare to use them to climb out while belayed by the climbers above.

Sometimes, there will be a ramp or narrow ledge along the wall of the crevasse that allows the fallen climber to walk out at one end. Of course, it is still necessary for the climber to remain tied to the climbing rope, until she is safely out of the crevasse.

Self-rescue by climbing out or using prusiks or ascenders can be the fastest and easiest way out of a crevasse, as well as the most effective method for small climbing parties to carry out a rescue. It is the *only* feasible method for a rope team of two. If self-rescue is not possible, and the fallen climber is in the crevasse only a short way, another option is for the rescue team to simply use their muscle power to haul out the fallen climber. Otherwise, the rescuers can use a pulley system to haul out the climber efficiently and safely.

"On the way to the summit, I fell into a crevasse on the Ingraham Glacier. I tried to step over it, but the rope went taut, I turned upside down, and fell in. There were five people on my rope team. I didn't go in too far. They were able to pull me out right away. But I lost my ice axe. The head guide was leading my rope. After they pulled me out, the guide said, 'Okay, take a deep breath and let's keep going.' But I had to check my harness, make sure I had doubled back the waistbelt, make sure I was okay. The guide said later that I babbled on for about 10 minutes. Then I went on and made it to the summit. Later, I realized that I had never been afraid of anything before, because this incident scared the crap out of me! The experience also taught me something important about myself—I can square-off in tough business or personal situations because I'm not afraid. To me, that's the value of climbing, as a teaching instrument."

—Amber M. Brookman

HEATHER'S FALL ON MOUNT MCKINLEY

Heather fell into a crevasse while leading an all-women's party on Mount McKinley in 1995. "I was wearing a pack and pulling a sled. It was my first lead on McKinley," she recalls. "We had all made the summit and were descending, coming down to 8,000 feet, which is a minefield as far as crevasses go. I was thinking, 'We're done'—I had let down my guard. I can now hear what the mountain was saying: 'There's a guide down there who thinks she's just going to waltz off this thing.' But, I wasn't listening.

"I was looking for a cache we had left before our ascent. When you leave a cache on McKinley, you connect three wands together with duct tape to make one long wand so that snowfall won't cover it up. I saw a wand off to the right. I looked at my altimeter and thought, 'It feels too early. I think it's farther down the glacier.' But this looked exactly like our wand, gray duct tape with black writing on it. Off I went, to the right.

"When I got to the wand, I looked around, thinking, 'I don't remember leaving our cache here.' I pulled up the wand and it was short. The hairs on the back of my neck stood straight up. Then I noticed other wands making an X that I hadn't seen before. I was on a huge snow bridge. The snow was mushy. I felt like I was standing there holding a grenade with the pin pulled.

"Cate Casson was guiding with me. We're both usually pretty instinctive. She was watching me like a hawk, and saw me pull out the wand. I put it back ever so carefully and took one step back, when suddenly the whole thing collapsed like a bombay door! I'm falling and I've got snow and the sled coming in on top of me. I'm thinking, 'You screwed up big-time.' I remember losing my hat and goggles and being really upset about that. But I hung onto my ice axe.

"I wanted out badly, fast. There was no bottom to this thing, it was the black abyss. The walls were pretty narrow, though, so I could place my feet on each side and stem and climb up a bit. I ditched my pack on the ditch loop, and I had my ascender handy, attached to my gear sling. We had been spaced the right distance apart, so when the two women on my rope self-arrested and stopped me, I only went in about 20 feet. I was very proud of them.

"I was wearing snowshoes, so I was able to use the ascender and climb up the wall of the crevasse to the lip. It was overhung, so Cate and our third guide, Emily, had to pull me up over the lip. Cate said, 'Don't *ever* do that again!' I don't plan to, but it was pretty satisfying to know that, even though I had made a mistake, we had all our ducks in a row and were doing everything right."

Climbers using a **Z-pulley** to "rescue" Francey. (Terry Austin)

In any rescue situation, to keep the rope from digging into the lip of the crevasse where it could hinder rescue efforts, slide a stationary object under it if possible. An ice axe laid parallel to the crevasse creates a smooth surface for the rope to pass over, but almost anything will work—a pack, ski, or ground pad. Be sure to anchor the implement to keep it from falling into the crevasse too. If the rope is already deeply cut into the lip, do your best to get something under the rope to prevent it from going in farther.

As soon as the rescue system is in place, each climber takes a position on the rope, and then either pulls hand over hand or walks slowly away from the crevasse. Whether using muscle power or a pulley system, exercise caution as the fallen climber approaches the lip of the crevasse, to prevent injury.

For demonstration, the guides elected to haul Francey out of the crevasse using a Z-pulley system. "The wall of the crevasse sloped inward, so I was able to rest my feet on a small ledge after they lowered me in about 25 feet," said Francey. "I couldn't see how deep the crevasse was, it was all broken up below me. Heather explained that very often what looks like the bottom can be a false floor. I could see the different consistencies of the snow and ice. In places, the wall was an icy blue. It was colder down there too. And quiet. To hear someone up top, they had to lean over the lip and call to me."

WHAT DO I DO WITH MY PACK?

It's a good idea to have what is called a ditch loop (an 8- to 12-inch perlon loop with carabiner) already attached to the haul loop on your pack. When you are traveling in heavily crevassed areas on a glacier and your pack is quite heavy, you can simply pick up the rope (or, if you're in the middle, both the rope trailing in front and behind you) and clip the rope into your ditch loop carabiner. If you fall into a crevasse, the ditch loop attached to the rope will hold you upright. Once in the crevasse, you simply take off your pack; it drops below you on the rope and acts as a weight on the end of the rope, making it easier to climb up.

You might be able to keep your pack on if the rescuing climbers are going to simply haul you out. Or, if you are going to climb out and there is another rope available in your group, you can send the pack up to the top on that rope.

THE CAUSE OF GLACIERS AND CREVASSES

• • • • • • • • • • • • • • • • • • •

Glaciers form on about 10 percent of the world's mountains, where heavy snowfall accumulates and freezes faster than it can melt away. Beneath the surface, the lower levels compact into hard ice. As tons of snow accumulate above, the glacial ice slowly moves over the terrain. As it flows over the bumps and curves of the bedrock beneath it, the surface of the glacier pops and cracks, forming crevasses.

When Terry's turn came to be "rescued," she took her camera with her. "I knew if I ever fell into a crevasse for real, the last thing I'd ever do is think to use my camera," she said. "So this would be my only chance to take photos from the vantage point of dangling in a crevasse. I backed off the lip and got lowered down about 30 feet on the rope. About 20 feet to my side was another climber dangling on another rope. We took photos of each other, and smiled bravely while waiting to be rescued. I also practiced using my prusik loops while they were setting up the pulley system."

By now you have realized that, in mountaineering, there is a lot of preparation centered around the possibility of disaster. Indeed, the mountaineer's credo is, "Prepare for the worst, hope for the best." If all this seems a bit daunting, trust that as you gain skill with tools and technique, you also gain confidence. Fear is a great motivator, and fear will keep you alert to danger. But experience will help rid you of unnecessary anxiety.

Francey and Terry emerged from crevasse-rescue training with a higher level of confidence. Terry was determined to try some ice climbing. At first, Francey was hesitant. She later stated, "I wasn't sure I'd have enough upper-body strength to climb out of the crevasse, and I was concerned about conserving my strength for the summit climb the next day. I finally realized that these were just mental reservations. How do I know if I can or can't do something unless I try? So, I did it. It was all part of my commitment to try some new experiences that would push me beyond my normal limits."

The guides and climbers dismantled the rescue ropes,

(continued on page 92)

Terry in crevasse with prusik slings in place.
(Heather MacDonald)

CREVASSE RESCUE

There are several ways to achieve crevasse rescue. Two methods are shown here, the C-pulley and Z-pulley systems. It is wise to study books written solely on crevasse rescue and to participate in as much training as possible to hone your skills for a variety of situations.

Any rescue attempt begins with setting an anchor or multiple anchors between the closest self-arresting climber and the crevasse. Multiple anchors are best, but even more important is the use of equalized anchors, where the load is distributed between a pair of anchors.

To create an equalized anchor using snow pickets, drive one picket into the ground, angling it

back about 45 degrees from the direction of pull to prevent it from popping out under tension. Be sure that the top of the picket meets the surface of the snow for greatest security (the picket should already have a webbing sling attached).

Drive in a second picket about 1 1/2 feet parallel to the first picket. Take a 3 1/2-foot piece of webbing and girth hitch it to the webbing already attached to the first picket. Then clip a carabiner to the webbing on the second picket and clip the 3 1/2-foot webbing to that carabiner.

Next, join the top and bottom part of the longer loop of webbing and tie an overhand knot

(continued on page 88)

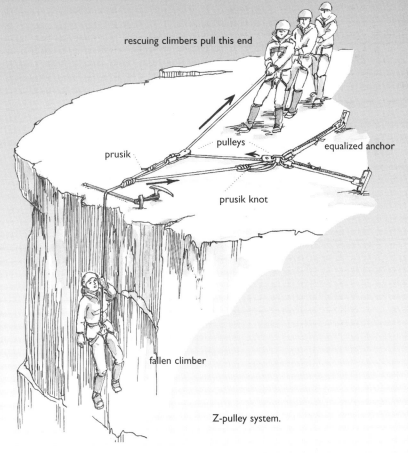

rescuing climbers pull this end

pulleys

equalized anchor

prusik

prusik knot

fallen climber

Z-pulley system.

CREVASSE RESCUE

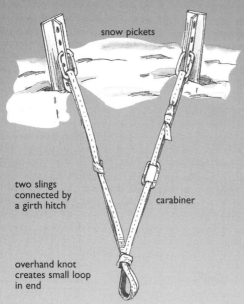

snow pickets

two slings connected by a girth hitch

carabiner

overhand knot creates small loop in end

Creating an equalized anchor.

(continued from page 87)

at that point. This knot will create a small loop in the webbing. Clip a locking carabiner to this loop. Tie a prusik onto the fallen climber's rope. Clip the prusik loop into the locking carabiner. If done correctly, the angle of the webbing that extends from both pickets should be about 30 degrees.

Slide the prusik knot toward the crevasse until the sling is tight. The load created by the weight of the fallen climber is now equally distributed to the pair of anchors. If one anchor should fail, the weight will be transferred to the other. At this point, the climbers still in self-arrest should be able to slowly release.

Another effective anchor is the deadman. First, at a safe distance from the lip of the crevasse, dig a trough. The depth will depend on the conditions of the snow pack, but the trough should be a minimum of 18 to 24 inches deep, parallel to the crevasse. Place a snow picket or ice

axe horizontally in the trough. Use a girth hitch to attach a sling (or *runner*) to the middle of the shaft of the picket or axe, and dig another trough that allows the sling to emerge smoothly toward the direction of pull. Cover the troughs with snow and pack it down. Clip a carabiner into the emerging end of the sling. This anchor can be used to secure a belayer or to attach to the rescue rope. It also can be used in conjunction with a snow picket or another deadman to create an equalized anchor.

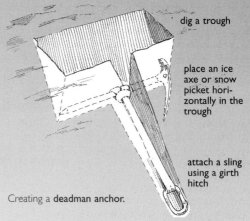

dig a trough

place an ice axe or snow picket horizontally in the trough

attach a sling using a girth hitch

Creating a deadman anchor.

As soon as you have anchored the climbing rope after a crevasse fall, you can begin to prepare a pulley system. The C-pulley system creates a quick and easy hauling system, especially good for climbers who haven't taken a deep fall into a crevasse. Also, if the climbing rope has already sawed into the lip of the crevasse, the C-pulley system allows the rescue climbers to use a separate piece of rope or even an entirely separate rope to execute the rescue.

To set up the C-pulley system, as soon as the climbing rope is anchored, place a pulley on the free end of the rope above the anchor. Clip a locking carabiner into this pulley, then send the pulley and carabiner to the fallen climber on a loop of rope. Keep hold of the slack end of the rope as you do so.

The fallen climber clips the pulley and the loop of rope into her harness with the carabiner. The rescuing climbers then haul on the rope to lift the fallen climber. Because the pulley creates a C-like curve in the rope, it is called a C-pulley system.

The Z-pulley system takes longer to set up than a C-pulley system, but it creates a greater mechanical advantage because it employs two pulleys (and ends up with two bends in the rope that look like the letter Z). This system is effective for hauling out a climber from a deep fall or retrieving an unconscious or injured climber.

To set up the Z-pulley system, place a rescue pulley on the rope at the anchor. Clip a locking carabiner to the pulley. Then attach the carabiner to the anchor slings. The second pulley is placed on the rope at a point closer to the crevasse. Instead of being attached to an anchor, this "free" pulley is clipped to a short sling that is also attached to the rescue rope with a prusik.

NOTE: If for some reason you have no pulleys, you can use carabiners. They will create more friction and make the rope harder to pull, but they will work in a pinch.

To use the Z-pulley system, the rescuing climbers pull the free end of the rope hand-over-hand. The rope should slide freely through the prusik knot near the anchor. If needed, a climber can be positioned at that anchor to keep the knot functioning.

As the rope is hauled in, the free pulley will move closer to the anchored pulley. Don't allow the two pulleys to get too close to each other, or you'll lose the load-transfer benefit of two pulleys. A belayed climber can reset the prusik on the free pulley by sliding it out again toward

the crevasse lip. Then you can begin hauling rope again, repeating this process until the fallen climber reaches the crevasse lip.

At that point, care must be taken not to injure or endanger the fallen climber by pulling her into the lip. She may have the strength to use her ice axe to pull herself over the lip while the rescuing climbers continue to maintain a taut rope. A belayed or anchored climber can approach the lip to assist the fallen climber. This is a good time to use the sitting bollard (see Chapter 6, page 69) to belay the assisting climber to the edge.

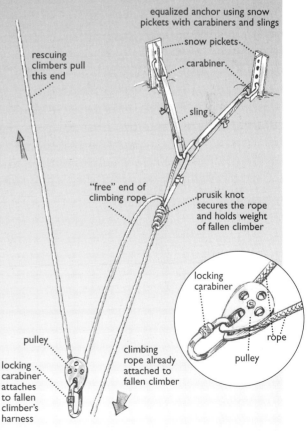

equalized anchor using snow pickets with carabiners and slings

snow pickets

carabiner

rescuing climbers pull this end

sling

"free" end of climbing rope

prusik knot secures the rope and holds weight of fallen climber

locking carabiner

rope

pulley

pulley

climbing rope already attached to fallen climber

locking carabiner attaches to fallen climber's harness

C-pulley system.

fallen climber

CLIMBING WITH PRUSIKS OR ASCENDERS

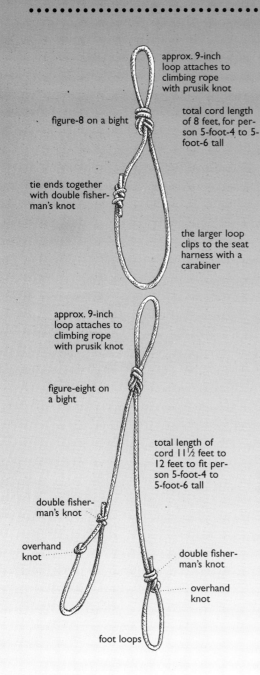

approx. 9-inch loop attaches to climbing rope with prusik knot

figure-8 on a bight

total cord length of 8 feet, for person 5-foot-4 to 5-foot-6 tall

tie ends together with double fisherman's knot

the larger loop clips to the seat harness with a carabiner

approx. 9-inch loop attaches to climbing rope with prusik knot

figure-eight on a bight

total length of cord 11½ feet to 12 feet to fit person 5-foot-4 to 5-foot-6 tall

double fisherman's knot

overhand knot

double fisherman's knot

overhand knot

foot loops

The Texas Prusik Sling.

When traveling on glaciers, always carry at least two prusiks or two mechanical ascenders. Some climbers carry both as insurance against loss of one or the other.

To make what is known as a Texas Prusik Sling, take about 20 feet of 6-mm perlon accessory cord and cut two lengths, one 12 feet long, the other 8 feet (these lengths are suitable for a person from 5-foot-4 to 5-foot-6 in height). The longer piece will become the sling for your feet. The shorter piece attaches your harness to the climbing rope.

Tie the ends of the short piece together using a double fisherman's knot. (See pages 56–59 for how to tie.) In this newly created loop, tie another 9-inch loop using a figure eight on a bight. This smaller loop will be attached to the climbing rope using a prusik knot. The larger loop clips to the seat harness with a carabiner.

In the longer piece of cord, create a foot loop at each end using a double fisherman's knot, backed up by an overhand knot to keep it from sliding down and tightening over your boots while climbing. In the middle of this piece, tie a 9-inch loop with a figure eight on a bight. This smaller loop will attach to the climbing rope with a prusik knot. To check that the prusik slings fit over your climbing boots and that they are the proper length for your height and reach, hang a rope from your garage rafter or a tree limb and attach the prusiks.

Many climbers go ahead and attach the prusik slings to their harness and climbing rope

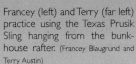

Francey (left) and Terry (far left) practice using the Texas Prusik Sling hanging from the bunkhouse rafter. (Francey Blaugrund and Terry Austin)

Using a Prusik Sling. 1. Sit in the seat harness, taking weight off the foot loops. Move prusik knot on foot sling up the rope as far as possible. 2. Then stand up. Slide the prusik knot attached to the seat harness up the rope as far as possible. Repeat the first step, and so on, until you reach the top.

before starting out. The trailing ends are stuffed into pockets, ready for use. An alternative is to use a carabiner to clip off the prusik to your harness or a gear sling without attaching it to the rope. It is still at easy reach, but not in the way when not in use.

To climb the rope to get out of a crevasse, remove the foot loops from your pockets or harness. Slip them over your boots. Stand up in the loops. Slide the prusik knot attached to the seat harness up the climbing rope as far as you can reach; it should be taut. Then, sit down in the seat harness, taking your weight off the foot loops. Move the prusik knot on the foot sling

up the rope, raising your legs as you go. Then stand up in the loops. Repeat the routine until you reach the top.

An alternative to carrying prusiks is to carry two mechanical ascenders on your seat harness with foot loops attached. The ascender replaces the prusik knot. The ascender locks onto the rope and employs a cam to grip the rope against backward or downward pull, but allows the ascender to be slid freely in the other direction. When in use, the climber remains tied into the climbing rope, and the ascender is attached to the climbing harness by a sling.

anchors, and pulleys, and moved to another spot where the crevasse offered a smooth, steep wall for ice climbing. The guides then anchored a few ropes again for climbing practice.

The basic ice-climbing techniques taught during the five-day seminar were designed to give climbers a taste of this vertical sport and to add a couple of techniques to their repertoire. The goal during the seminar is to teach *front-pointing*—or climbing ice using the front points of the crampons, your ice axe, and an ice tool (e.g., an *ice hammer*—a tool with a pick on one end and a hammer head on the other). Even if you plan not to pursue vertical ice climbing on a regular basis, the technique will come in handy any time you encounter a moderate-to-steep slope or an ice wall that requires front-pointing to ascend.

During training, Terry said, "I really was a little afraid of ice climbing. I saw one of the guides lower himself down the ice wall and then climb back up fast using his crampons, ice axe, and ice tool, and I thought, 'Oh, sure, Mr. Upper-body Strength. How about those of us with Olive Oyl arms?' I noticed he was pressure-breathing, though. When he came up over the lip, Heather said, 'That pumps you right up, doesn't it?' She had just done it herself and said that it was tough."

Terry continued, "The guides told us not to hold the shaft of the ice tool or ice axe too tightly or it would wear out our arms right away. We could hang by our wrist loops if we had to, to rest a bit, once we got a firm hold. They said, 'Careful not to smack your nose!' I thought I'd never remember all the tips because I knew I'd just be clinging by the skin of my teeth on this wall. . . . I started to get really nervous. Then the thought came to me that this couldn't be much harder than tree climbing, where you free-climb through branches to the top of the tree. I can do that. I trusted the tree-climbing equipment. I was on a rope for this ice climbing, and I had crampons and ice tools.

Top: Ice climbing; Terry front-points on the ice wall. (Heather MacDonald) **Above:** Ice hammer.

ICE-CLIMBING TECHNIQUES

To climb vertical or steeply sloped ice walls, use the technique called front-pointing, with crampons, an ice axe, and ice hammer. Start with your feet about shoulder width apart. First, plant the picks of the ice tools in the wall. Reach up as high as you can and out slightly to the side, to prevent chips of ice from hitting you. Planting the pick in the wall doesn't take much force unless you are on exceptionally hard ice. A quick flick of the wrist is usually enough to plant the pick, rather than drawing back from the shoulder and slamming the pick into the wall. Avoid hacking and chopping at the ice to achieve a good hold. A well-placed, concise swing conserves energy and will help you maintain balance when perched on the wall.

As soon as both tools are placed in the ice at the same height overhead, let your weight pull down a bit on the axe and hammer while you kick the front of each crampon into the wall, one foot at a time. Keep your heels level or dropped down slightly, and your legs straight. If you raise your heels, the front points of the crampons will pop out of the ice.

Let your legs do the work. Don't pull yourself up with your arms only. To conserve energy, hang from your wrist loops with arms straight rather than grasping the tools with your arms bent.

To ascend the wall, first replant the ice tools one at a time. Pull them out of the wall by levering up and down, rather than side to side. Then replant your feet—again, one at a time. Repeat this process slowly, efficiently, methodically. If a tool or foot pops out of the ice, replant it quickly, remembering to keep your heels down. If you swing out to one side (an effect of loss of balance called "the barn door"), attempt to regain position as soon as possible.

The person belaying you should maintain tension in the rope to prevent you from falling.

As you ascend, the belayer will pull in rope as needed, allowing no slack to build in the rope.

The universal communication for climbing on belay was developed by Paul Petzolt, the founder of the National Outdoor Leadership School. When the belayer is ready to belay, she says to the climber, "Belay on." As the climber begins to climb, she says, "Climbing." If the climber needs slack, she says, "Slack." If there is too much slack in the rope, the climber says, "Up rope," and the belayer pulls in the slack. If the climber suddenly falls, she yells, "Falling!," just as in self-arrest. When the climber reaches her goal and is secure, she says, "Off belay." The belayer responds, "Belay off." Falling objects should be identified immediately with a shout of "Rock!" or "Ice!" to warn climbers below.

There are other communication parameters. Study them carefully and practice with a friend until they become second nature to you.

Francey prepares to plant ice hammer and ice axe as she moves closer to the lip. Note that her heels are down to maintain the foothold. (Heather MacDonald)

RAPPELLING

If a slope is too steep to descend facing forward, or facing into the slope, a rappel may be necessary. The technique is simple but can turn into a dangerous endeavor if not done correctly. A rappel involves an anchor, a rope, friction on the rope (through a belay device or wrap of the rope), and the climber. The rope is tied off to the anchor while the climber lowers herself down the cliff. In some cases, the rope or two joined ropes are threaded behind an anchor (e.g., a tree or a bollard) so the rope can be pulled for the next rappel. Your safety relies on your ability to control your speed on the rope. Once mastered, most climbers enjoy rappelling. As one climber said to me, "It's the quickest way down a mountain, short of falling."

The beginning mountaineer should first learn to rappel without using a belay device, to get a feel for the dynamics of controlling friction and body weight. Friction is created when you pass the rope through the carabiner on your waist harness and wrap the rope around your hips. One hand stretches forward to guide the rope; the other hand becomes the brake hand, held closely to your side or—on very steep slopes—behind your back against your hip.

Keep your feet apart, your knees bent. Try to relax. Your body should lean back comfortably from the slope (don't lean too far or you might flip over). To be able to see the route, turn a little toward the braking hand. Don't bounce or leap down the face of the cliff. Move slowly and steadily to avoid putting extra stress on the anchor.

If you encounter an overhang, drop below it slowly. You'll be suspended on the rope below it, and you might twist or spin. Continue down slowly. As soon as your feet touch the cliff again, you will regain footing.

Climber **rappelling**. Brake hand remains against the hip. Body is slightly turned toward brake hand for better visibility.
(Keith Gunnar)

So I finally relaxed a little. When it came my turn to be lowered into the crevasse, it wasn't as hard to climb out as I thought it would be. My foot slipped out a couple of times, and so did my ice axe, but the guide was belaying me from up top, so I didn't fall. I tried to center my balance around one tool while moving the other one."

Francey added, "I was surprised at how much power I had when I used the equipment the way I was supposed to. My arm muscles had been stretched to new limits, but I was glad that I had gone ahead and discovered that I could do it."

Each time the guides demonstrated a technique, they explained why that technique was used, Francey recounted. "They gave us real-life examples of why *not* to do something, the examples usually ending in the story of someone's death. They kept emphasizing how important it was to learn from others' mistakes so that we wouldn't have to go that route."

Terry added, "Everything we learned was very stimulating and illuminating, and gave us more confidence. Whenever I'd start to get nervous, I'd remind myself of one of my favorite sayings—'Worry is a misuse of the imagination.' But when you're standing there, looking into a crevasse, you're really not imagining it!"

After the day's training, the climbers hiked back to Camp Muir for a hearty dinner. Then it was early to bed, with hopes for a summit bid the following day. The weather system that had visited the mountain that morning was still hanging on. On Mount Rainier, storms can vanish as quickly as they appear or stay for days, like unwanted guests.

How would Mount Rainier treat its climbing guests? Heather would rise at 1 o'clock the next morning to check the weather. If the weather had intensified and visibility was poor, the summit climb would be cancelled and the climbers would spend the day learning more technique on the lower flanks of the mountain. If visibility were good and the wind somewhat calm, the climbers would leave the warmth and safety of their bunks before sunrise, and venture to the top of the mountain that was currently their world.

Chapter 8

SUMMIT DAY

It's show time!" Heather's voice reverberated in the predawn silence of the bunkhouse. Three o'clock had come quickly for Francey, Terry, and the other climbers, most of whom had lain awake during the night or slept fitfully in anticipation of summit day.

"I think one reason most of us were awake all night is because we all were trying to stay hydrated, so it seemed that somebody was getting up to go to the privy about every 10 minutes," said Francey. "When I got up to take my turn, as I rounded the corner to the outhouse, there it was—the summit, glowing white against the clear midnight sky. I'll never forget the sight. I knew then that we would be given the opportunity to test ourselves."

The night before, Heather had given the climbers the rundown on summit-day procedure. "Have your harness next to your bunk, ready to go. Put your headlamp on your helmet, ready to go. Crampons, ready to go. Two full quarts of water, ready to go. Put your lunch in your pack, ready to go.

"Also in your pack, bring all the clothes you have that will keep you warm. No cotton tees or shorts. Throw in an extra pair of socks. If you drop a mitten, you can wear a sock on your hand. Bring your down parka, sunglasses, ski goggles. All your layers of gloves, a warm hat, a sun hat.

"If your headlamp uses a 4.5-volt battery, put a fresh one in it. If you're using AA batteries, take an extra set because the cold saps the power in no time."

Heather's clothing recommendation was to start with two layers: a base layer with pile jacket and pants on top. "Save the Gore-Tex parka and pants for windy or nasty conditions. Gore-Tex is slick. The pile doesn't slide as easily. When you first go outside, you'll feel a little chilled. Don't worry, you're probably going to be just right once we get moving. If you go outside and feel toasty warm, you're probably overdressed."

"Down parkas should be kept in the top of the pack," Heather said. "When we head into a rest break, you're going to walk right up to the person in front of you on the rope. As you walk, that person will coil in the rope. You'll turn and do the same thing for the person coming up behind you. We stay tied in to the rope at all times. After you coil in, take off your pack, pull out that down parka, and put it on. Then eat and drink. Conserve the heat you just built up by climbing. You'll save energy by not having to cool down and warm up, over and over again. Just before we leave the break, take off the down parka and stuff it back into the top of your pack. I never climb anywhere without my big down parka."

Heather encouraged everyone to try to eat something in the morning before leaving the bunkhouse. "Also, drink a half-quart of water. Fuel your system." She added, "Try to go to the bathroom here in the outhouse before we leave. If you have to take a leak on the mountain, you'll stay on the rope and do it. Tell your guide. If you have to do something more serious, we use what we call a blue-bag system. Deposit your waste in the blue plastic bag. We carry the empties up, you carry the full ones down. We try to keep this mountain clean."

Terry later commented, "This tidbit of advice might have been the real reason for the general lack of sleep that night. Everyone was worried that they'd have to use 'the blue bag.'"

Heather estimated that it would take a little more than six hours to reach the summit, weather allowing. "I'll be setting the pace," she said. "Everyone should be able to keep up. It might seem a little fast to some, a little slow to others. But everyone should be able to make it. We want to travel in the early part of the day. Later in the afternoon, it becomes less safe to travel on the mountain, when the snow gets soft and we begin to see avalanches and rock fall."

The planned route would take the climbers across the Cowlitz Glacier, up and over Cathedral Gap, onto the Ingraham Glacier, and onto Disappointment Cleaver.

"I was so impressed with the guides. They are so capable and extremely patient. Their work must be like raising different children each week, having to start with a new group, teach them how to walk all over again, protect themselves, be alert to danger, and encourage them to do their best. With all my backpacking experience, I thought I knew how to conduct myself in the mountains, but once we hit the glacier, it was a whole new ballgame."

—Terry Austin

HIGH-ALTITUDE RELIEF

Performing normal bodily functions in an abnormal situation—such as perched on a mountainside—is always a challenge. However, there's no avoiding it, especially since you must be generous in fueling and hydrating yourself in order to maintain energy and prevent altitude sickness. The first time you pee or defecate in front of your rope team is the worst. Just ask them to kindly turn their heads away. Then it's all downhill . . . no pun intended.

The first time I had to relieve myself on a climb, I actually enlisted the help of a fellow climber (and friend) to squat in front of me, shielding me from view of other approaching climbers. Yes, it was embarrassing, but when you gotta go . . . and in time, I returned the favor to her.

Here are a few tips to help you over the hurdle of outdoor sanitation.

Urinating can be done in several ways. At night, in the comfort of your tent, you can use an empty water bottle designated for this purpose. Make sure you have identified the bottle clearly. If you are using a "base camp" to stage your climb, consider digging a pit into which all climbers in your group can relieve themselves, thus minimizing the impact on your surroundings. Otherwise, pee onto the snow far away from the snow you plan to melt for drinking water. Some women use a device that funnels urine through a tube and onto the ground or into a bottle. I don't care for such devices for two reasons: it's something else to carry, and it's a stinky thing to carry!

Some women's mountaineering apparel (such as from Marmot and L.L. Bean) includes a zippered or pull-apart crotch that allows you to relieve yourself without having to disrobe—assuming all layers of your apparel are built this way. You can confine this feature only to your thermal underwear, then remove only outer layers to accomplish your duty and still remain somewhat covered.

Solid waste requires a disposal technique. Lacking a hole or privy, the best method is the "blue bag system," so named for those blue opaque plastic garbage bags that also come in black, brown, and white. Use whichever color you prefer! The idea is to defecate directly onto the snow, ice, or rock, then put your hand in a small plastic baggie and use it to pick up the waste and toilet paper. Deposit this small baggie in your larger, sturdier "blue bag" and secure with a twist-tie. If you are having your period while climbing, follow the same blue bag disposal procedure for used tampons and pads. Because the collected waste will usually freeze, you won't notice much of an odor while carrying it off the mountain for proper disposal. On high, remote mountains, such collected waste is often jettisoned into a deep crevasse instead of being carried back to civilization.

Use baby wipes to keep yourself clean, as it's doubtful that you'll have enough melted snow in which to bathe. Although you can use clumps of snow to give yourself a "snow bath," I wouldn't recommend doing this on private parts.

A special note about relieving yourself while in full mountaineering gear: Here is where the split crotch concept really shines, as you should not have to remove your harness to perform. If you don't have the split crotch clothing system, make sure you do have a harness with adjustable, buckled leg loops. Then the harness waist belt can stay fastened—and you can remain securely fastened to your rope team—while you pull down your pants in response to Nature's call.

Crossing the Ingraham Glacier at sunrise. (Keith Gunnar)

"We'll take our first break on the Ingraham Flats at about 11,000 feet. It will take us a little over an hour to get to that spot. Then we'll wind our way across the glacier and get on the Cleaver."

Heather spoke reassuringly. "You'll see some exposed rock. Don't let that throw you. You've got crampons on and you're on rock? No big deal. You know how to rest-step, you know how to pressure-breathe. Try to find the best rhythm you can. Don't let it throw you mentally. To the rest break at the top of the Cleaver at 12,300 feet takes about an hour and 40 minutes.

"After that, we'll wind our way up the Ingraham Glacier and take our next break at 13,400 feet. From there, it's about an hour to the summit. At times, we've stayed on top for up to an hour when the weather is nice. If the weather's bad, we just touch the crater and head back down. Maybe take time for a couple of hero shots, maybe not."

The guides have a saying, which Heather now shared with the group: "'The ascent is optional; the descent is mandatory.' If you get yourself up there, you gotta be darn sure you can get yourself down. A lot of people reach the summit and yell, 'Yay, the climb is over!' Nope. It's only half over."

Heather elaborated: "On the descent, you're tired, you tend to let down your guard. But you need to pay attention. You can't run on empty. This is when most mountaineering accidents happen, on the way down. It should take us three-and-a-half hours to get back down to Camp Muir. We take four breaks going up, including one on the summit, and two breaks on the way down— one at the top of the Cleaver, the other on Ingraham Flats."

Heather encouraged the group to stay mentally psyched. "I think everyone can climb this mountain. Sometimes, you have a bad day. Tomorrow, if any one of you is having a bad day, or feel this is not your cup of tea, that's fine. There are a couple of ways we can deal with that. We can send a guide down with you. Or, weather permitting, there are safe spots on the mountain where we can put a person in a sleeping bag, sometimes in two sleeping bags, and then continue climbing while they sleep or watch the sun come up, and wait for us to come back down and pick them up. It may seem a little inhumane, but it's not that bad."

And then she related the good news: "The route is in great shape, not too broken up. The main thing is, the mountain has to say 'Yes.' The weather has to be good. We have to be able to see and to stand on our feet."

Heather ended the evening by reading a passage from *Mt. Analogue: A Novel of Symbolically Authentic Non-Euclidean Adventures in Mountain Climbing*, by Rene Daumal: "You cannot stay on the summit forever. You have to come down again. So why bother in the first place? Just this: What is above knows what is below. But what is below does not know what is above. One climbs, one sees, one descends, one sees no longer but one has seen. There is an art in conducting oneself in the lower region by the memory of what one has seen higher up. When one can no longer see, one can at least know."

After Heather left, Terry laid awake in her sleeping bag. "I kept wondering if I had everything packed. I was already wearing my base layers and wool socks. The rest of my clothes were ready to slip on. I knew I only had to put in my contact lenses, eat, and go. I went over my mental list a few times and still couldn't sleep. People were snoring. So, I put in earplugs and finally dozed off. I dreamed that I didn't hear Heather come in and tell us to get up. Everyone else was ready and standing outside. Someone suddenly asked, 'Where's Terry?' They all had to wait an hour for me to get ready. After that dream, whenever someone opened the door to go out to the bathroom, I'd jerk awake, thinking it was Heather. When she finally did come in at 3 A.M., I was awake and ready."

Francey also had a dream about Heather. "I was drinking so much water that I had to get up and pee about four times during the

"**A**t the first rest break, I told one of the guides that I felt too exhausted to breathe harder. He said, 'It's the opposite of what you think. If you exhale forcefully, it will energize you. Push all that air out of your lungs to make room for more oxygen.' I started doing that on the next stretch and visualizing the lung-capacity test we have to take at work every year. Then I started thinking about Greg and our dogs and all my friends and family who were thinking about me. I remembered a favorite quote: 'That which doesn't kill you makes you stronger.'"

—Terry Austin

• •

"The journey is what matters.
The summit is an arbitrary
place to turn around."

—Heather MacDonald

• •

Francey (left) and Terry (right) bundled up at the rest break on top of Disappointment Cleaver. (Heather MacDonald)

night. I had a hard time getting warm. First, I changed my socks and then took them off, put on my down booties, and wrapped my feet in one of my fleece shirts. I slept in everything I was going to wear on summit day. I probably had too many layers on and couldn't warm everything up. I felt like a little mouse on a wheel, going 'round and 'round.

"When I finally got warm, I fell asleep and dreamed that I asked Heather if she thought I could really climb up Disappointment Cleaver because I was really worried about it. In my dream, Heather told me that it was rocky and steep, but that we were roped together and I wouldn't have any problem. She told me not to worry about it. Before we'd turned in that night, I had debated with myself whether or not to ask Heather. I didn't, so instead she came to me in my dream and helped me deal with it. I felt more relaxed then, drank some more water, went out to pee, then crawled back into my sleeping bag and fell right back to sleep. I slept about an hour and a half, then woke up around 2 A.M., and couldn't go back to sleep. Just waited for the door to open. I still remember hearing the door open and Heather's first footfall. The door swung open, hit the table behind it, and Heather exclaimed, 'It's show time!'"

Indeed, the show was about to begin. As Heather lit the propane lamp, she announced, "It's clear, I can see the summit. We're going."

Francey recalled, "It seemed that everyone else had been lying there, waiting, because everyone got up at once, like we were firefighters ready to go to a fire. I finished dressing, even put on sunscreen. Then I drank another quart of water and ate a fruit bar. I was ready."

Terry gobbled some instant oatmeal with a handful of raw almonds and drank a cup of tea while getting dressed. "I was rushing around, putting in my contacts, and I heard someone moan, 'I think I'm going to be a blue-bag boy today.' Another said, 'I'm going to avoid that like the plague.' Typical guy talk at three in the morning!"

By 4:30 A.M., the climbers were roped up and heading up. Their headlamps created a string of lights from Camp Muir across the Cowlitz Glacier. The sky was clear and the early-morning air

• •

"**W**e took our heart rates. One of the climbers noticed that his was elevated and asked Heather about it. She said it was pretty normal and that once you become acclimated, it would drop back to normal. So we started taking our resting heart rates every morning and evening. Heather told us that hers is normally around 80. Mine was running 68 to 72. Francey's was between 80 and 84. One of the guides said that his resting heart rate at sea level is 55 and at Camp Muir, 55."

—Terry Austin

• •

was exceptionally cold, near zero degrees. Luckily, there was no wind to intensify the cold.

"I was so thankful that Francey was in front of me and that Heather was leading our rope," Terry said. "I felt energy from them. There was another climber, Ted, behind me and then Claire, one of the cooks from Camp Muir."

They reached the first rest break on the Ingraham Flats a little before 6 A.M. "I was ready to stop for a break," said Terry. "The sun was just beginning to come up. I was still in a sleepy fog and it seemed like I was dreaming this part of the climb. We put on our down parkas, sat on our packs, and tried to force down food and water. I saw the guides huddled together, talking. Something was up."

One of the climbers had decided to turn back. He had climbed the mountain a couple of seasons ago, but confessed that he hadn't trained as hard for this climb. The cold had taken a toll on his energy.

"When he turned around, I wondered if that was going to happen to me too," said Terry. "We had to sit there while the guides switched people around so that one of them could go back with him. I started getting cold."

Francey ignored the drama of the turning climber. "I was trying to focus on eating and drinking, and I was also taking in the beauty of the dawn. My mouth was dry from pressure-breathing. I was very focused on my breathing. I tried to eat some of my sandwich, but it didn't taste very good. I tried a granola bar, but it was frozen, so I went back to the sandwich and drank more water. My toes were a little cold, but I felt good, physically and mentally. I had no problem hiking the rocky trail over Cathedral Gap. That made me more confident about Disappointment Cleaver. I knew now that it would be a piece of cake, because Heather had said so in my dream."

Francey and Terry later related their climb of the Cleaver. "We went up the nose, the steepest part, but supposedly the safest way," said Terry. "My legs started feeling like lead. I began taking a pressure breath about every three steps, then one pressure breath with every step. On a couple of really steep sections, I had to break my stride to step over a boulder. I started to lag a little and pulled on Francey."

"I felt the pull, but it didn't affect my forward motion," Francey said. "The rope was getting taut now and then. I'd pace myself to make sure that Terry didn't feel like she was getting pulled."

"Francey was like a robot in front of me, so good at rest-stepping and breathing," Terry added. "I was trying so hard to do that and started to psych myself out. I had no sense of time, just one foot, then another foot, breathe, breathe. Ted encouraged me. He'd say, 'Good job,' or 'You own that rest step.' I thought, 'Can I keep this up for the next three or four hours?'"

Terry said she never looked up. "I knew it would be too daunting to see another steep section above me after just having completed one. The trail seemed to level out a bit, just when I needed it.

• •

"**I** had made the commitment to see this through and hopefully overcome some of my imagined fears—of being cold, of falling, of failing. As I focused on actually doing what I came here to do, and gained skill and knowledge, those fears diminished and I knew I had what I needed to make this journey a success."

—Francey Blaugrund

• •

There was one really steep, icy section. I had slowed down, using both arms, pushing off rocks or snow on each side of me. Heather yelled down from above, 'Terry, stand up and breathe!' I thought, 'I *am* breathing!' Then she said, 'Don't pull on Francey.' I thought, 'Oh my God, I'm blowing it.' I kept going, trying to stand up straighter. At last, we reached the top of the Cleaver and our rest break. That stretch almost pushed me beyond my limits."

Francey snuggled in next to Terry, to help her get warm. "It was real breezy above the Cleaver," Francey recalled. "We stayed there longer than normal because two more people were turning back for Camp Muir. While the guides rearranged the ropes, we all started feeling cold from sitting there so long. To help keep Terry warm, I rummaged around in my lunch sack and pulled out a Milky Way candy bar. It was frozen. I bit off a piece and gave it to her."

"Francey saw me shivering and could tell I was worried," said Terry. "The guy sitting in front of us was shaking really hard. One of the guides had given him a down parka, but he was still shaking with cold. The guides huddled again, talking logistics.

"It was right there, I could see it clearly just ahead of me. The last few steps, just a little higher, and then there was nothing. The end of the ridge, and then nothing but that clear, empty air. I stopped climbing. . . . I was standing on the top of the world."

—Stacy Allison (on Mount Everest),
Beyond the Limits

"The guy shivering in front of me said, 'I don't want to be a liability, so maybe I should go back down.' That made me think, 'I'm freezing, too; I wonder if I'm going to be a liability.' Heather walked by, so I asked her, 'Heather, do you think I can make it?' She said, 'Yeah, just breathe harder. You're breathing like you're sitting on the couch. Just push that air out and breathe harder than you've ever breathed in your life.'

• •

"**W**hen I climb, I visualize myself as an arrow, heading up."

—Heather MacDonald

• •

"I thought, 'If Heather believes I can do it, then I can make it.' I just didn't want to ruin the climb for anyone else. Heather told us that the next section was going to be about the same, but the steep parts wouldn't be as long. That's good, those steep sections just kicked me in the ass. She told me again, 'Just breathe, that is the key. I know you can do it.' I was so relieved, knowing she had faith in me."

Francey had conquered her nemesis, the Cleaver. "I felt the hardest part was done," she said. "The psychological fear of the Cleaver was gone. I wasn't concerned about the rest of the climb.

"The sun was getting bright and we could see the rest of the mountain. Little Tahoma peak was visible below us, mantled in a row of clouds shaped just like it. Pinks and blues filtered through the clouds, the snow almost glittered. The snow was packed hard, icy in many places. We could see another party about 20 minutes ahead of us. They were on route to the summit, wa-a-a-y up there. They looked like a line of ants. I realized we were going up there too. I felt confident because I had learned so much during the past two days."

Terry also was awed by the scenery unfolding in the daylight. "Glaciers, broken pieces of ice blocks, and crevasses lay below us. We were above the clouds, as though in an airplane, looking down on all this. I had no idea that it would be this extreme. I felt like I was in the pages of *National Geographic*. A negative thought—'I should have hiked the bleachers more!'—sneaked into my mind, but I pushed it aside and focused on taking one step at a time and breathing harder than I had ever breathed in my life."

When they finally left the rest break, Francey concentrated on following the footprints of the climber in front of her. "The only time I looked around was at a rest stop, or if we had to wait for somebody on the rope, or when Heather was placing a wand on the route. I actually had two or three hot flashes on the way up! It was a comfortable feeling, made me warm all over except in my toes. I wasn't worried about getting to the summit. I knew if I kept eating, drinking, and breathing—and not looking over the edge—I would be fine. The focus that I had developed by rest-stepping and pressure-breathing from the time we had left Paradise for Camp Muir propelled me up the mountain."

At one point on the next stretch, Terry wondered, "Why the hell wasn't anyone behind me breathing as hard as I was? Then I thought, 'Who cares what they're doing? I just have to do what I have to do to get to the top.' I visualized us on top. I wished I had my camera to capture the scenery, because nobody was going to believe this. But it was deep in my pack and there was no way I could stop. I just focused on stepping and breathing, stepping and breathing. It became almost like a meditation."

Francey also got into a rhythm of rest-stepping and pressure-breathing, and saying a mantra, "'Love and joy, love and joy.' Each time I looked to the side or stopped saying my mantra, I'd fall off pace and have to refocus on breathing and walking."

"In certain really narrow sections, the trail was just the width of my foot and straight down was rock and ice," said Terry. "Greg would never believe where I was, even if someone showed him photos. I started thinking about Greg's brother Jeff, who had died last year after a long painful illness. How he never complained. I wasn't in pain, but it made me wonder what Jeff must have gone through. I realized how lucky I was to be healthy and doing this. I knew that Jeff and others were there in spirit with me, helping to push me to the top. I just kept going."

As they neared the rest break at 13,400 feet, Francey finally looked down. "We hiked around a hump and the trail leveled off a little, it wasn't as steep. The sun was fully out and you could see the hard ice under the light cover of snow. It looked slick all the way down to the buckled glacier and exposed crevasses. They looked like humongous buildings that had toppled

Top: Francey and Terry's rope team nears the rest break at 13,400 feet. **Above:** Francey and Terry's rope team approaches the summit. (Heather MacDonald)

over and broken up. I was amazed to look down and realize I wasn't scared, and to see the immensity of the mountain, and realize that we had already hiked through all of this safely. I was kind of getting into this climbing."

The wind had come up, whipping around the climbers, pushing and pounding them. "I became a little tense because a couple of times, if I didn't brace myself with my ice axe, I nearly got blown over," Francey said. "I remember what one of the breast-cancer survivors on Expedition Inspiration said, how sometimes you have windy days in your life and you just have to be strong and get through them. I almost started crying because I was suddenly aware of how much I was

Above: (left to right) Francey, Heather, and Terry on the summit of Mount Rainier. (Terry Austin)

The summit at last! (Heather MacDonald)

learning and how fast it was all unfolding before me. I was saying 'Yes' to a new experience. I was healthy and strong and able to use all my strength to get through this."

Terry recalled that she kept waiting at rest breaks for one of the guides to say, "That was the hardest part, you've done it, the rest is easy." It didn't happen.

"I was on the edge the whole time," she said. "I'd make it through one section, put that behind me and concentrate on the next one. I kept thinking, 'I'm not dying, I feel strong. This is just hard work.' At the last rest break, I looked at my watch and it read 9:35 A.M. It seemed like we'd been through so much already and here it was only 9:35! I said to Francey, 'I'll never be able to look at 9:35 in the morning in the same way again.'"

At the high rest stop, the wind continued to batter the climbers and visibility grew poor. Temperatures began to drop. There was urgency in Heather's voice. "The next stop is the top. Put on your Gore-Tex jackets. It's going to be colder and windier once we round the summit ridge."

The summit ridge! Could it be that close? Many climbers have turned just below this and other summits in conditions too dangerous to warrant proceeding. In 1996, I had turned around at this same high point on Mount Rainier. Increasing wind and a ground blizzard were conspiring to take away our visibility and footing. So we turned. To retreat from your goal when you're so close is sometimes a painful decision, but often a wise and safe one.

Heather had told the climbers to be prepared for the wind as they neared the summit. As she rounded a curve and headed up a steep pitch, Francey started taking more pressure breaths between steps. "I felt the rope grow taut. I put up my hand to let the climber in front of me know that I wasn't able to go any faster. Farther along, I saw this big rock up ahead. I thought, 'What's up with these rocks?' The wind was taking my breath away and knocking me off balance. Then I realized Heather

Summit sisters Terry and Francey. (Ted Curcio)

was standing by that rock, coiling in the rope. I was at the summit and didn't realize it.

"I started getting teary, but suppressed it and began coiling in the rope, reeling in Terry. When our rope team was coiled in, Heather said, 'Good job, you made it, we're at the summit. Now take off your packs and get those down parkas on.' I leaned against the hill and was sitting down. That's how steep it was."

Terry recalled, "We left the high rest break at 10 o'clock. Heather said it would take about an hour to get to the summit from there. At one point, I had to look at my watch; it read 10:35. Then we started passing people coming down from the summit. Nobody said anything except, 'Congratulations.'

"I figured it would take another half-hour. I looked up and was shocked to see Heather and Francey coiling in the rope. It was so cold and so windy, it was hard to believe I

"**A**t last we stood on the rim of the big crater, where the wind was blowing so strongly we could hardly keep our footing, and oh, it was bitter cold. . . . We hastened on to the great high knob and at 4:30 P.M. on August 10, 1890, we stood on the tip top of [Mount Rainier]. It was a heavenly moment; nothing was said—words cannot describe scenery and beauty, how could they speak for the soul! Such sensations can be known to only those who reach the heights."

—Fay Fuller, first woman to summit
Mount Rainier, from *Leading Out*

After the climb, a congratulatory hug for Terry and Francey from Lou Whittaker.

was there. Francey and I shared a big hug. We started to cry, then laughed when we realized that our tears were freezing on our eyelashes! Then we hugged Heather and got out the camera for a couple of quick shots. And we finished off Francey's Milky Way."

As soon as the other climbers reached the summit, Heather announced, "It's going to be touch and go, the wind is getting worse, we've got to get out of here. Take a couple of photos and let's pack up and head down."

The descent went smoothly. When the climbers walked into the rest break above Disappointment Cleaver, they walked out of the clouds and into sunshine. At Camp Muir, the climbers who had turned around on the mountain were waiting with congratulatory handshakes and hugs.

"I felt so energized and alive. We did it, and we were safe," said Terry. "Francey and I hugged, laughed, and cried again. It reminded me of the Joni Mitchell lyric, 'Laughing or crying, you know it's the same release.'"

"I had never felt so much elation," said Francey.

"And pride," Terry added, "I felt as proud as though I had climbed Mount Everest."

Chapter 9

OTHER MOUNTAINS, OTHER JOURNEYS

Congratulations! You've completed a basic mountaineering course, albeit vicariously, through the experiences of Francey, Terry, and other women who have journeyed forth to explore the higher reaches of the planet and the limits of their psychological and physical abilities. Along the way, they have confronted fears and encountered obstacles, both real and imagined. In experiencing the beauty and power of the mountain, they have discovered joy and strength.

Francey and Terry made the summit of Mount Rainier, but you may not be so fortunate. Turning short of a summit is a normal part of mountaineering—it happens all the time, in fact. If you want to enjoy a long career of mountaineering, avoid the "summit-at-all-costs" mentality, which is a sure ticket to disaster. There is no way to control weather, snow, and ice conditions. There is no way to fend off death if you become ill at altitude and refuse to descend. Turning around is what keeps you alive. The mountain will still be there if you want to try again.

In 1998, Heather returned to Mount Everest and led a client to 28,000 feet before she and the expedition leader called a halt and decided to turn. They might have made it to the summit, but the rapidly deteriorating weather would surely have turned the descent into a life-threatening struggle. Heather later said that she was "devastated" to have to turn at 28,000 feet, but again, "it was the right decision." Mount Everest is unfinished business for Heather. She plans to return, to climb the mountain "in style"—meaning a round trip.

Above: Heather preparing a tent platform at Camp V (25,000 feet) on Mount Everest. **Left:** Heather MacDonald on Mount Everest. (Heather MacDonald)

Yes, the summit is the goal, but even a thwarted journey can provide high drama and many lessons, as 26-year-old Jennifer Herzig and her climbing partner, 22-year-old Leah Hall, discovered during an attempt on an unclimbed peak in the Yukon, in the St. Elias range.

A bush pilot dropped off the two women on the Chitna Glacier. "At first look, it appeared to be smooth, but when we started walking, we discovered that the glacier was more unconsolidated and broken up than we expected," says Jennifer. "We knew the pilot would not be back for us for 14 days. That left just the two of us in the middle of the Yukon, no radio contact.

"When I fell into the first crevasse, I only went in up to my armpits and was able to get myself out. I didn't see it at all. We were in an ice-fall area where crevasses aren't as easily read. We had been taking a rest break. I started walking to stretch out the rope and popped through with 40 feet of slack between me and Leah. As soon as she saw me go in, she ran the other way, to take up the slack, and self-arrested. After I got out, we realized that we were in extremely unconsolidated snow conditions. The weather was unusually warm, the snow bridges weren't holding up at all. We decided to wait until nightfall, hoping that the snow would freeze and consolidate so that we could move out of the area. We sat on a ledge for 12 hours, waiting to travel safely. Leah remarked, 'I've never been in this situation before. It's almost like being on top of a rock climb without a rope.'

"We were finally able to travel around one in the morning. Leah took an extremely brave lead all the way back to the flats. She probed every step. Ironically, when we got back to the flats, where we felt safer, she suddenly fell through another hole, but was able to get herself out. We could hear water running in the bottom. I was wearing snowshoes, and it looked like I could step across. I said, 'Leah, just help me get across this and we'll switch leads.' I stepped up to the lip, thinking it was just one big step across. But it was wider than I thought, and I went in.

• •

"To transcend the everyday and allow yourself a separation from everyday ritual, to gain a different perspective, to be freed up to think differently and experience life on a larger scale, you become attuned to the elements, respond to them and touch the infinite."

—Barbara Harris

• •

Jennifer Herzig digs out a tent platform on the Chitna Glacier. (Leah Hall)

"For almost a minute, I couldn't feel anything under my feet, couldn't get a foothold. That was freaking me out. I started moving my arms, yelling 'Help me!' but I just knocked more snow down on top of myself. Leah was in self-arrest on top. I finally got my feet on something solid. I kept thinking, 'I don't want to die like this, this would be a horrible way to die.'

"I finally got control of my ice axe and was able to find the wall and get my feet up in front of me. I shouted to Leah that I didn't think I could get myself out. Because the snow was so soft, she was able to maintain self-arrest and use one hand to grab two pickets out of her pack and punch them into the snow, creating an equalized anchor. We already had a prusik attached to the rope, making it easy for her to clip into the anchors. As soon as she knew that the anchor was going to hold, she stood up and made a deadman with her ice axe as a third anchor. Then she set a Z-pulley system and started hauling me out. All this took her about 10 minutes. We had practiced for this possibility.

"I kept thinking there was no way she was going to be able to pull me out on her own. I had to help myself. While she was busy setting up the pulley, I started knocking down the snow above me so I could get a better look at the lip. When the pulley was ready, I stemmed the wall—put my left foot behind me and my right foot in front—and as I stood up, Leah pulled. It only took a few pulls and I was out. I crawled all the way to Leah. We embraced and just bawled, we were so exhausted. We set up our tent right there and sat through eight days of warm weather, waiting for this minefield of crevasses to freeze solid so that we could get out of there. We had to ration our food the last four days. I led back to camp, which helped me get my confidence back.

"I was disappointed not to have a chance at the summit, but I don't regret the decision. I learned more about myself—and about courage, and self-reliance, and having the right climbing partner—on that trip than on any other climb. As human beings, we earn our experiences."

Clearly, mountains can be places for joy and self-discovery, and they also can be dangerous and unforgiving. A climber must earn every step on the journey to and from the summit, whether following a guide or on one's own. Physical and mental conditioning are crucial to success, not to mention an enjoyable outing. As in life, if you are not prepared for the challenge that lies ahead, you are more likely to fail—or, in the least, to have a miserable outing.

When you venture out, you'll have your own experiences. And, like these women, you will have the opportunity to conquer fears and surmount obstacles as you accumulate skills and experience. Some fears will remain intact, and obstacles will continually appear in your path. Both are there to challenge you, to keep you alert, as you follow your chosen route.

At journey's end, you may be able to answer the question, "Why climb?" In the least, I hope you will have fun. As in most endeavors, you get back what you put into an adventure.

To close this book, I would like to talk about two of my own mountaineering experiences. After climbing on Rainier four times, I signed up for a trip to climb 19,870-foot Huayna Potosi in Bolivia. Climbing above our 18,000-foot high camp thrust me into a new world of rarefied atmosphere and advanced climbing techniques, including the use of a fixed rope up the steep summit headwall.

Fixed ropes are commonly used on difficult routes for safer and speedier climbing. One long line of rope, made especially for this use, or one or more climbing ropes are anchored to the route and left there while climbers ascend and descend. The climbers move up and down the rope using an ascender, which is attached to the climber's waist harness by a sling. As a safety backup, a

passing an intermediate anchor

Using a **mechanical ascender** on a fixed rope. (Separate harness sling not shown for clarity.)

separate sling is also attached to the harness, then clipped to the rope with a carabiner.

Because there are intermediate anchors along the rope, it is necessary for the climber to stop at each anchor, unclip the safety carabiner, and reattach it on the other side of the anchor, then do the same with the ascender. Never detach both at the same time.

In addition to climbing the summit headwall on a fixed rope, our group also enjoyed the experience of kicking steps or buckets into the wall for footholds. The sensation was similar to vertical ice climbing, except that we had one hand on the ascender, the other on the ice axe, and our feet in depressions in the wall.

Whenever a climber approached an anchor, he or she would call out, "Anchor!" and the rest of the group would stop while the climber detached and reattached his or her safety carabiner and ascender. It was slow going, but our entire group made it to the summit—and back down—safely.

For my next "big" mountain, I chose the "Roof of Africa," Mount Kilimanjaro. I

Andrea Gabbard (standing, facing camera) on Mount Kilimanjaro with friends.

had heard a lot about the trip, which was considered a strenuous high-altitude trek rather than a technical climb. I was attracted by the prospect of passing through many different temperate zones on the trek, from dry African savanna, to rain-forest jungle, to heather forest, to high-altitude desert and glaciated summit. Especially enticing was the prospect of a four-day game-viewing safari in Kenya, following the climb.

An extinct volcano, Kilimanjaro rises 19,340 feet from the floor of Tanzania. We followed the less-frequented Machame Route and encountered only three other parties during the six days spent on the mountain. Although crampons, ice axe, and rope travel were not required, my other mountaineering skills of pressure-breathing, rest-stepping, staying hydrated, and generally taking good care of myself served me well. I summited with ease and felt very strong the entire time.

Our climbing group was composed of nine women and three men. Seven of us achieved the summit. At Uhuru Peak (where a rustic sign proclaims, "You are now at Uhuru Peak, the highest point in Africa"), I stood beside my friend and climbing mentor, Peter Whittaker, and the other

climbers whose friendship and dedicated physical effort had made this journey one of my most memorable. Gazing out at the clouds covering the vast African continent and feeling strong despite the effects of the thin air, I knew that this summit day—and the courage and camaraderie that had made it possible—would remain with me forever, becoming a place to which I could return time and again in my heart.

That is why I climb.

Andrea Gabbard on summit of Mount Kilimanjaro (19,340 feet), "The Roof of Africa."

Chapter 10

RESOURCES

BOOKS

Inspiration from Women Who've Led the Way

Allison, Stacy, with Peter Carlin. *Beyond the Limits: A Woman's Triumph on Everest*. New York: Delta Books, 1993.

Blum, Arlene. *Annapurna: A Woman's Place*. San Francisco: Sierra Club Books, 1983.

Chisholm, Margo, and Ray Bruce. *To the Summit: A Woman's Journey into the Mountains to Find Her Soul*. New York: Avon Books, 1997.

da Silva, Rachel (editor), Arlene Blum. *Leading Out: Women Climbers Reaching for the Top*. Seattle: Seal Press, 1992.

Daumal, Rene, Roger Shattuck (translator). *Mount Analogue: A Novel of Symbolically Authentic Non-Euclidean Adventures in Mountain Climbing*. Boston: Shambhala Pocket Classics. (Currently out of print.)

Evans, Laura. *The Climb of My Life: A Miraculous Journey from the Edge of Death to the Victory of a Lifetime*. San Francisco: Harper Collins, 1996.

Gabbard, Andrea. *No Mountain Too High: A Triumph Over Breast Cancer*. Seattle: Seal Press, 1998.

Gould, Jean. *Season of Adventure*. Seattle: Seal Press, 1996.

Kocour, Ruth Anne, with Michael Hodgson. *Facing the Extreme: One Woman's Story of True Courage, Death-Defying Survival, and Her Quest for the Summit*. New York: St. Martin's Press, 1998.

Mazel, David (editor), *Mountaineering Women: Stories by Early Climbers*. College Station, TX: Texas A&M University Press, 1994.

Olds, Elizabeth Fagg. *Women of the Four Winds: The Adventures of Four of America's First Women Explorers*. Boston: Houghton Mifflin Company, 1985.

Robertson, Janet. *The Magnificent Mountain Women: Adventures in the Colorado Rockies*. Lincoln, NE: University of Nebraska Press, 1991.

Thayer, Helen. *Polar Dream*. New York: Simon & Schuster, 1993.

More Mountaineering

Chouinard, Yvon. *Climbing Ice*. New York: Random House, 1982.

Graydon, Don, and Kurt Hanson. *Freedom of the Hills*, 4th ed. Seattle: The Mountaineers Books, 1997.

Lowe, Jeff. *Ice World: Techniques and Experiences of Modern Ice Climbing*. Seattle: The Mountaineers Books, 1996).

Molenaar, Dee. *The Challenge of Rainier*. Seattle: The Mountaineers Books, 1979.

Schullery, Paul (editor). *Island in the Sky*. Seattle: The Mountaineers Books, 1987.
NOTE: This book is entirely about Rainier; it contains Fay Fuller's article, "A Trip to the Summit."

Whittaker, Lou, with Andrea Gabbard. *Lou Whittaker: Memoirs of a Mountain Guide*. Seattle: The Mountaineers Books, 1994.

Taking Care of Business

Getchell, Annie. *The Essential Outdoor Gear Manual: Equipment Care & Repair for Outdoorspeople*. Camden, ME: Ragged Mountain Press, 1995.

Howe, Steve (editor). *Making Camp: The Complete Guide for Hikers, Mountain Bikers, Paddlers & Skiers*. Seattle: The Mountaineers Books, 1997.

McGivney, Annette. *Backpacker's Leave No Trace: A Practical Guide to the New Wilderness Ethic*. Seattle: The Mountaineers Books, 1998.

Miller, Dorcas S. *Good Food for Camp and Trail: All-Natural Recipes for Delicious Meals Outdoors*. Boulder: Pruett, 1993.

Wellness . . .

Gill, Paul G., Jr., M.D. *The Ragged Mountain Press Pocket Guide to Wilderness Medicine and First Aid*. Camden, ME: Ragged Mountain Press, 1997.

Isaac, Jeff. *The Outward Bound Wilderness First-Aid Handbook*, revised ed. Rockville, MD: The Lyons Press, 1998.

Tilton, Buck, and Frank Hubbell. *The Wilderness First Responder: A Text for the Recognition, Treatment and Prevention of Wilderness Emergencies*. Old Saybrook, CT: Globe Pequot Press, 1998.

. . . and Safety

Armstrong, Betsy R., and Knox Williams. *Avalanche Book*. Golden, CO: Fulcrum Publishing, 1992.

LaChapelle, E.R. *The ABC of Avalanche Safety*, 2nd revised ed. Seattle: The Mountaineers Books, 1995.

McClung, David, and Peter Schaerer. *The Avalanche Handbook*. Seattle: The Mountaineers Books, 1993.

Moynier, John. *Avalanche Awareness: A Practical Guide to Safe Travel in Avalanche Terrain (Mountain Safety)*. Evergreen, CO: Chockstone Press, 1993.

Selters, Andy. *Glacier Travel and Crevasse Rescue*. Seattle: The Mountaineers Books, 1990.

MAGAZINES AND WEBSITES

Climbing Magazine
Climbing, Inc.
1101 Village Road, Suite LL-1B
Carbondale, CO 81623

Phone 970-963-9449
Fax 970-963-9442
email: climbing@climbing.com
www.climbing.com

allmountain.com
A mountain and mountaineering specialized research engine.
www.allmountain.com

eClimb
email:info@eclimb.com
www.eclimb.com

GORP: Great Outdoors Recreation Pages
www.gorp.com

GreatOutdoors
611 South Congress Avenue, Suite 350
Austin, TX 78704
Phone 512-416-5035
Fax 512-707-0181
email: info@greatoutdoors.com
www.greatoutdoors.com

The Mountain Zone
911 Western Avenue, Suite 302
Seattle, WA 98104
Phone 206-621-8630
Fax 206-621-0651
email: info@mountainzone.com
www.mountainzone.com

Rock & Ice
PO Box 3595
Boulder, CO 80307-3595
Phone 303-499-8410
Fax 303-499-4131
email: editor@rockandice.com
www.rockandice.com

Views from the Top
"The premier hiking and climbing webzine"
www.lexicomm.com/views/index.html

WSPN.net
"A complete source for women's sports"
www.WSPN.net

IN GOOD COMPANY: CLUBS AND AFFILIATIONS

The American Alpine Club
710 Tenth Street, Suite 100
Golden, CO 80401
Phone 303-384-0110
Fax 303-384-0111
www.americanalpineclub.org

The American Mountaineering Center
710 10th Street, Suite 110
Golden, CO 80401
Phone 303-384-9145
amcntr@ix.netcom.com

Becoming an Outdoors-Woman
Dr. Christine Thomas
College of Natural Resources
University of Wisconsin-Stevens Point
Stevens Point, WI 54481
www.state.nj.us/dep/fgw/bowhome.htm

Earthwise Journeys
A woman-owned company specializing in women's trips that are run by responsible tour operators and outfitters. Features backpacking and trekking trips in the U.S., Canada, Europe, Latin America, and elsewhere.
PO Box 16177
Portland, OR 97292
Phone 503-736-3364
email: earthwyz@teleport.com
www.teleport.com/~earthwyz/women.htm

National Park Service
1849 C Street NW
Washington, DC 20240
Phone 202-208-6843
www.nps.gov

Tread Lightly
298 24th Street, Suite 325
Ogden, UT 84401
Phone 800-966-9900
Fax 801-621-8633
www.treadlightly.org

Women Climbers Northwest
A non-profit organization formed to promote climbing/mountaineering and other wilderness activities among women.
PO Box 31223
Seattle, WA 98103-1223
email: wcn@scn.org
www.scn.org/rec/womenclimbers

Women in the Wilderness
Washington Outfitters & Guides Association
704 228th Avenue NE
Redmond, WA 98053
Phone 425-392-6107
Fax 425-392-0111
email: Debbyhorse@aol.com
www2.ool.com/women/wwwboard/messages/198.shtml

Women's Outdoor Network
PO Box 50003
Palo Alto, CA 94303
Phone 650-494-8583
Fax 650-712-9093
email: wonforfun@earthlink.net
home.earthlink.net/~wonforfun

Woodswomen
Woodswomen is a non-profit educational organization open to all women, offering a variety of activities, including mountaineering.
25 West Diamond Lake Road
Minneapolis, MN 55419-1926
Phone 800-279-0555
Fax 612-822-3814
www.woodswomen.mn.org

STRENGTHENING SKILLS

Mount Rainier Instruction and Guiding

Summer:
Rainier Mountaineering, Inc. (RMI)
Paradise, WA 98398
Phone 360-569-2227

Summits Adventure Travel
51902 Wanda Road
Eatonville, WA 98328
Phone 360-569-2992

Winter:
Rainier Mountaineering, Inc.
535 Dock St., Ste 209
Tacoma, WA 98402
Phone 253-627-6242

Other Instructional Schools

Alpine Ascents International
121 Mercer Street
Seattle, WA 98109
Phone 206-378-1927
Fax 206-378-1937
email: aaiclimb@accessone.com

Exxum Mountain Guides
Grand Teton National Park, WY
Phone 307-733-2297

International Mountain Climbing School
North Conway, NH
Phone 603-356-7064
email: guides@ime-usa.com

National Outdoor Leadership School
288 Main Street
Lander, WY 82520
Phone 307-332-4784/6973
Phone for Leave No Trace:
800-332-4100
Fax 307-332-1220
email: admissions@nols.edu
www.nols.edu

Outdoor Skill Development
2926 Lantz Avenue
San Jose, CA 95124
Phone 408-371-0261
www.jthomas-osd.com/index.htm

Outward Bound
National Office
Route 9D
RR 2 Box 280
Garrison, NY 10524-9757
Phone 800-243-8520

Fax 914-424-4000
www.outwardbound.org

**SOLO: Stonehearth Open
Learning Opportunities**
*Offers wilderness and emergency medi-
cine courses on a variety of skill lev-
els, with lots of hands-on practice.*
RR 1, Box 163
Conway, NH 03818
Phone 603-447-6711
email: solo@stonehearth.com
www.stonehearth.com

Wilderness Medicine Institute
PO Box 9
Pitkin, CO 81241
Phone 303-641-3572

Wilderness Medical Associates
RR 2, Box 890
Bryant Pond, ME 04219
Phone 207-665-2707

Avalanche Schools and Seminars

Alaska Avalanche School
Alaska Mountain Safety Center,
Inc.
9140 Bresters Drive
Anchorage, AK 99516
Phone 907-345-3566

American Avalance Institute, Inc.
PO Box 308
Wilson, WY 83014
Phone 307-733-3315

**Canadian Avalanche Training
School**
P.O. Box 2759
Revelstoke, B.C. VOE 2SO
Phone: 604-837-2435
Fax 604-837-4624

**National Avalanche
School/National Avalanche
Foundation**
133 S. Van Gordon Street, Suite
100
Lakewood, CO 80228-1706
Phone 303-988-1111

National Avalanche Center
PO Box 2356
Ketchum, ID 83340
Phone 208-622-5371
(recorded message 208-788-1200
ext. 8027)
Fax 208-622-3923

Silverton Avalanche School
San Juan Mountain Search and
Rescue
c/o San Juan County Sheriff's Office
Silverton, CO 81433
Phone 970-387-5531

**Sierra Ski Touring Winter Skills
Series**
P.O. Box 176
Gardenville, NV 89410
Phone 702-782-3047

AVALANCHE CONDITIONS

*For information on local avalanche
conditions:*

CALIFORNIA
Angeles Mountains/George Duffy
Phone 818-335-1251

Lake Tahoe/Donner Summit Area
(Truckee)
Phone 530-587-2158

San Bernardino/Ron Huxman
Phone 909-383-5700

Central Eastern Sierra
(Mammoth Lakes)
Phone 760-934-6611

Mount Shasta/5th Season Shop
Phone 916-926-3606 or 5555-

COLORADO
Rockies: Denver/Boulder
Phone 303-275-5360

Rockies: Fort Collins
Phone 970-482-0457

Rockies: Colorado Springs
Phone 719-520-0020

Rockies: Vail
Phone 970-827-5687

Rockies: Aspen
Phone 970-920-1664

Rockies: Durango
Phone 970-247-8187

IDAHO
Smoky, Sawtooth, and Pioneer
Mountains
(Ketchum)
Phone 208-788-1200 ext. 8027

MONTANA
Northwest Montana Rockies
(Whitefish)
Phone 406-257-8402

South Central Mountains
(Bozeman)
Phone 406-587-6981

Southern Mountains
(Cooke City)
Phone 406-838-2341

Southern Mountains
(West Yellowstone)
Phone 406-646-7912

NEVADA
Ruby Mountains
Phone 702-753-6867

NEW HAMPSHIRE
Tuckerman Ravine
Phone 603-466-2725

NEW MEXICO
Sangre de Cristo Mountains
Phone 505-776-2291

OREGON
Southern Washington Cascades
and Mount Hood area
(Portland)
Phone 503-326-2400, 503-808-2400

UTAH
Sundance/Mount Timpanogos Area
(Provo)
Phone 801-378-4333

Tri-Canyon Area
(Salt Lake City)
Phone 801-364-1581

Park City Area
(east of Tri-Canyons)
Phone: 801-649-2250

Mt. Ogden south to Tri-Canyons
Phone 801-626-7400

North Wasatch
(Logan)
Phone 801-797-4146

La Sal Mountains
(Moab)
Phone 801-259-7669

WASHINGTON
Cascades and Olympics
Phone 206-526-6677

WYOMING
Teton, Wyoming, and Wind River
  Mountains
(Teton Village)
Phone 307-733-2664

CANADA
(www.avalanche.ca/snow)

ALBERTA
Phone 403-243-7253 ext. 7669
Toll-free 1-800-667-1105
www.avalanche.ca/snow

Banff National Park
Phone 403-762-1460

BRITISH COLUMBIA
Phone 604-290-9333
Toll-free 1-800-667-1105
www.avalanche.ca/snow

Canadian Rockies
Phone 403-243-7253 + snow
  (7669)

IN GENERAL, ON THE INTERNET
Avalanche Forecasts and
  Information
www.nwac.noaa.gov

Cyberspace Snow and
  Avalanche Center
www.csac.org

Westwide Avalanche Network
www.avalanche.org

WOMEN'S WELLNESS
The Melpomene Institute
*A clearinghouse of research and
  information on women and exercise, while pregnant, during
  menopause, etc.*
1010 University Avenue
St. Paul, MN 55104
Phone 612-642-1951
Fax 612-642-1871
email: melpomen@skypoint.com
www.melpomene.org

EQUIPMENT AND CLOTHING CHECKLIST

EQUIPMENT

(total cost: $2,200–$2,800)

Backpack
Sleeping bag
Ground pad/inflatable mattress
Tent
Harness
Rope
Perlon cord
Ice axe
Ice hammer
Ice screws
Pickets
Carabiners

Rescue pulley
Ascenders
Belay device
Plastic mountaineering boots
Crampons
Helmet
Headlamp, extra batteries
Glacier glasses with side shields
Goggles
Defogger
Topographical maps
Compass
Altimeter
Hiking poles

CLOTHING / PERSONAL GEAR

(total cost: $1,700–$2,000)

Hooded weatherproof parka
Weatherproof pants or bibs
Hooded down-insulated parka
Fleece or pile jacket
Fleece or pile pants or tights
Lightweight/heavyweight thermal
Underwear
Wool socks
Warm hat with ear coverage
Synthetic fabric liner gloves
Fleece or wool gloves or mittens
Weatherproof outer gloves or mittens
Waterproof gaiters

Down booties
Balaclava
Sun hat or ball cap
Cotton bandanna
Synthetic fabric sport bra and panties
Lightweight nylon or polyester shorts
First aid kit
Baby wipes
Plastic baggies
Biodegradable toilet paper
Hairbrush or comb
Toothbrush, toothpaste
Sunblock, sunblock lip gloss
Bowl, spoon, mug
Water bottles

OPTIONAL

Water purification device or tablets
Earplugs
Camera, extra batteries, film

Journal, pencil
Paperback book

Index

Credits and Permissions

Illustrations by Elayne Sears.

All photographs courtesy Andrea Gabbard, unless noted otherwise.

Photos on pages 11, 19, 27, 49, 63, 115, and 120 by Cliff Leight.

Photos on pages 33, 80, 96, and 109 by Keith Gunnar.

Quotes from *Beyond the Limits: A Woman's Triumph on Everest,* by Stacy Allison with Peter Carlin, published by Little, Brown and Company, New York City, 1993. Reprinted by permission of the publisher.

Quote from *Facing the Extreme: One Woman's Story of True Courage, Death-Defying Survival, and Her Quest for the Summit,* by Ruth Anne Kocour with Michael Hodgson. Permission requested from St. Martins Press.

Quote from *Annapurna, A Woman's Place,* by Arlene Blum, Sierra Club Books, San Francisco, 1983. Reprinted by permission of the publisher.

Quote from *To the Summit: A Woman's Journey into the Mountains to Find Her Soul,* by Margo Chisholm and Ray Bruce. Permission requested from Avon Books.

Quotes from Maureen O'Neil, Arlene Blum, and Fay Fuller, which appeared in *Leading Out: Mountaineering Stories by Adventurous Women,* edited by Rachel da Silva © 1992, 1998, Seal Press. Reprinted by permission of the publisher.

Quotes from Fay Fuller in "A Trip to the Summit," reprinted from *Island in the Sky,* by Paul Schullery © 1987, with permission of the publisher, The Mountaineers, Seattle, WA.

Quote from *Mount Analogue: A Novel of Symbolically Authentic Non-Euclidean Adventures in Mountain Climbing,* by Rene Daumal, translated by Roger Shattuck. Permission requested from Shambhala Pocket Classics.